SAMUEL BECKETT

MODERN MASTERS

MODERN MASTERS

EDITED BY frank kermode

samuel
beckett

a.alvarez

NEW YORK | THE VIKING PRESS

Grateful acknowledgment is made to Grove Press, Inc. for
permission to quote from the following by Samuel Beckett:
"Dante and the Lobster," a story from
More Pricks Than Kicks, All rights reserved.
Watt, All rights reserved.
Murphy, first published in 1938.
Molloy, Malone Dies, The Unnamable,
Copyright © 1955, 1956, 1958 by Grove Press, Inc.
How It Is, Copyright © 1964 by Grove Press, Inc.
Waiting for Godot, Copyright ©1954 by Grove Press, Inc.
Endgame, Copyright © 1958 by Grove Press, Inc.
Eh Joe, Copyright © 1967 by Grove Press, Inc.
Krapp's Last Tape, All That Fall,
Copyright © 1957 by Samuel Beckett,
Copyright © 1958, 1959, 1960 by Grove Press, Inc.
"Whoroscope," a poem from *Poems in English*,
Copyright © 1961 by Samuel Beckett.

IN MEMORY OF SETH HOLT
1924 – 1971

CONTENTS

SAMUEL BECKETT

Introduction: Absurdity and the Absurd

When *Waiting for Godot* was first produced in Paris in 1953, Samuel Beckett was approaching fifty and virtually unknown. Although he had been publishing for nearly a quarter of a century, he had few books to his credit. In 1929 he had contributed to a coterie collection of homages to James Joyce, *Our Exagmination round his Factification for Incamination of Work in Progress*, one of those books which seem, even at the planning stage, to have been destined to be a collector's item. Throughout the 1930s he had published sporadically and always in the same overbred way: a short and polemical study of Proust; two remarkably slim volumes of poetry; a book of short stories with a fighting title, *More Pricks Than Kicks*; and in 1938 a comic novel called *Murphy*. All had sunk more or less without trace. Shortly after the war, in 1947, he had published his own French translation of *Murphy*, which sold 95 copies in the first four years. At the beginning of the 1950s, when

Beckett's name began appearing more frequently in Paris —*Molloy, Malone Meurt, L'Innommable*, and *En Attendant Godot*, all originally written in French, were published between 1951 and 1953—Beckett was still known only to the most devoted connoisseurs of the avant-garde. Yet in 1969, only sixteen years after the first Paris performance of *Godot*, Beckett was awarded the Nobel Prize for literature. More important and more improbably, he was one of the few Nobel choices about whom nobody argued; Beckett's right to that usually questionable laureateship was unquestioned and obvious. He was a recognized world figure, an authority, a major influence.

Yet, even now his total output is still relatively small and is becoming, as it were, even smaller; it is also forbiddingly difficult and certainly becoming more difficult. These two qualities, in fact, go together; his recent play, *Breath*, staged just before he received his Nobel Prize, requires no actors and lasts for thirty-five seconds; his most recent novel, *Lessness*,[1] runs to fourteen small pages of large print and features one immobile figure in a landscape of ruins. Beckett is an artist of great originality and even greater purity who has steadily refused to make any concessions whatsoever to his public. The larger his reputation has grown, the chillier and more formidable his work has become and the further he personally has retreated into the shadows. Apparently he has always been a martyr to shyness, prone to painful silences in social situations; since he has become famous his diffidence and reticence have increased. He shies away from publicity as vehemently as Buster Keaton shied away from the camera in Beckett's one film—called *Film*—which is itself an allegory of shyness, transforming Bishop Berkeley's *esse est percipi* into dra-

[1] *The Lost Ones* was published after *Lessness* but written before.

matic terms, as though to be perceived were the greatest agony. Beckett gives no interviews, is never seen around, and keeps to his own small band of devoted friends. The biographical details are hard to find and often contradictory. When the news of his Nobel Prize broke, Beckett could be reached neither in his Paris apartment nor in his cottage in what he calls the "Marne mud." He was finally run to ground in a Tunisian hotel, where, again like Buster Keaton, he was besieged by a small army of international journalists. Without success. Although they waited for days, they glimpsed not an eyeball, not a single hair of him. Needless to say, he did not go to Stockholm to accept the prize.

Despite the obscurity of his work and the obscurity of his personal life, despite the fact that he has written plays without actors, acts without words, and novels without plot or punctuation—in short, despite the fact that there is no easy or obvious nook on which the general public can hang its hat—Beckett is one of the world's most famous living writers, certainly the most famous living playwright. Clearly he is not the most successful commercially; plays by more popular playwrights whom he has influenced, like Harold Pinter, almost certainly do better at the box office, while a Broadway phenomenon like Neil Simon probably earns more in twenty-four hours than Beckett does in a year—and I do not romantically underestimate Beckett's earnings. Nevertheless, every casual theatergoer knows about Beckett and has an opinion of his work. Beckett is the man who wrote a play that changed the whole of contemporary theater: it was about two tramps waiting nowhere in particular for someone who never shows up.

Waiting for Godot and *Endgame* have become standard repertory classics. But they represent only the tip of the Beckett iceberg. The submerged mass consists of works for the theater, for radio, and works in prose (it is misleading to call the latter novels) of extreme difficulty and compression. I am not convinced that they are read any more frequently or more willingly than was, say, Sartre's impregnable *Being and Nothingness* at the height of the fashion for existentialism. Except, of course, by the academics, for whom the discovery of Beckett in the late 1950s was providential.[2] By that time the New Criticism, the close analysis of texts considered as objects utterly separate from their creators, seemed more or less to have outlived its usefulness. A new mode of intensely autobiographical poetry was beginning to emerge, less ornate, less opaque, less immediately resistant to the reader, and it made many of the careful New Critical skills seem somehow redundant. In comparison, Beckett's concentrated, learned, and allusive work, and his insistence on separating his writing from his life, seemed ideal. Moreover, he came with the highest possible reference: he had once been associated with James Joyce, crowned king of Modernism and the Alexandrian style, to cope with whose work the New Criticism had largely been forged and on which it had been patiently honed. Not surprisingly, Beckett's work is now surrounded by great mounds of commentary, much of it rubble of interest to literary archeologists, but not to the ordinary reader for whom I am writing. John Calder, the British publisher of Beckett's nondramatic writing, has said: "More books have been

---

[2] According to Melvin J. Friedman, the French were the first to plant their flag in Beckettland. That was in the early 1950s and it culminated in Alain Robbe-Grillet's study of *Godot* in 1953. After that, as in Indochina, the Americans took over from the French: "Then American critics, who have since virtually usurped the field from the French, started to explore the labyrinthine corners of Beckett's work—and the period of neglect was at an end" (*Samuel Beckett Now*, ed. Melvin J. Friedman [Chicago and London, 1970], p. 7). After nearly two decades, the American presence is still large, but there is as yet no sign of Beckett's capitulating.

written on Christ, Napoleon and Wagner, in that order, than on anyone else. I predict that by A.D. 2000 Beckett may well rank fourth if the present flood of Beckett literature keeps up."[3] It is a gloomy prospect.

For the nonspecialist, the endless commentaries and commentaries on commentaries may induce only a muffled despair, but he accepts it all as a sign of Beckett's importance. For everyone, including the Nobel Prize Committee, Beckett is *the* artist of deprivation and terminal depression, and he has expressed his vision of desolation with unique power. He has pushed all the way through to the end—logically, emotionally, artistically. One does not need to have read every word he has written to admire the courage and purity of his effort, to identify with it, and to recognize the cost.

In the first days of his fame Beckett was usually bracketed with Ionesco as a dramatist of the Absurd. This was understandable but misleading. Ionesco's *The Bald Soprano*, which was first produced in Paris in 1950, three years before *Godot*, was not only a smash hit—it was still running twenty years later, like Agatha Christie's *The Mousetrap* in London—it was also a turning point, the first genuinely antitheater theater. Ionesco took the successful formula for light comedy and stood it on its head. He used the conventional middle-class drawing room for his setting and conventional clichés for dialogue—culled, in fact, from a language primer. The result was both put-on and discovery. The platitudes, so remorselessly swapped by two model British families, were subtly doctored into madness, so that what began as a joke finished as the poetry of banality, absurdity in the most literal sense of the then fashionable term. When Camus talked of the Absurd in *The Myth* of *Sisyphus*, he meant a life lived solely for its own sake

[3] *Beckett at 60* (London, 1967), p. 2.

in a universe that no longer made sense because there was no God to resolve the contradictions. In other words, what Camus called Absurd, Kierkegaard—more Christian, more precise, and even less optimistic—had called Despair. But for Ionesco, Grand Master of the Theater of the Absurd, absurdity was what it usually is: raging, hilarious farce.

Beckett, however, is an Absurdist in the strict, appalled sense that Camus intended. He has created a world in which Godot never comes and Mr. Knott lives up to his name, in which it seems perfectly natural to pass one's time in an urn or a dustbin, up to the neck in sand or face down in the mud, a world which, seen from the skull-like room of *Endgame*, is devastated, postatomic, and so empty that a solitary human being seems like a monstrous intrusion. Absurdity in Ionesco's more obvious sense appears only on the side, as the obsessional calculations by which his characters plot and predict and so make safe every eventuality, as the vaudeville patter with which they ritualize their relationships, and as the occasional vaudeville calamities— the pratfalls and collapsing trousers—which they stoically endure. Absurdity in this sense is a by-product of their metaphysically absurd condition; it is the best they can hope for, the worst they always expect.

No doubt the superficial resemblances between Beckett and Ionesco made it easier for the public, already softened up by the latter's more taking brand of Absurdity, to accept Beckett's stringent vision. Yet the final difference between the two writers is radical and profound. Unlike Beckett, who maintains a mollusk-like taciturnity in the face of all criticism, Ionesco has always been a controversialist, unable to resist the temptation to justify and explain himself in interviews, articles, and tetchy letters to the editor. In recent years he has even published his notebooks, in which he comes on unconvincingly as a deep thinker. Yet in practice his genius lies not in his profundity but in his ability to create dramatic images that are as immediate, as affecting, and as irredeemably strange as dreams, and then to let them work themselves out with a dream's irrational but compulsive logic. He makes it seem perfectly normal for there to be rhinoceroses in the street or a corpse growing in the bedroom. Everything makes sense yet is beyond reason. He once remarked to an interviewer:

> The dream is pure drama. In a dream, one is always in mid-situation. . . . I think that the dream is a lucid thought, more lucid than any one has when awake, a thought expressed in images, and that at the same time its form is always dramatic.[4]

At his best, Ionesco has been true to his dreams. He almost never creates characters of any depth or substance; the people in his plays are sudden and two-dimensional, like the figures in a dream. And, as in a dream, the complexity is all in their immediate situation. He has put his nightmares on stage, unadulterated and with an uncanny sense of what works in that tight space framed by the proscenium arch. The result is pure nihilism. After all, what can survive when the placid façade of middle-class life splits open and the submerged fantasies come pulsing through? There is a curious intensity in Ionesco's best plays · the tone may be farcical, yet the effect is single and unhesitating, like that of a lyric poem.

Ionesco's dream world is unpredictable, irrational, and abrupt. Beckett's is the opposite: it is the world of chess, meticulous and utterly rational. Appropriately, one of his finest plays is called *Endgame*, and the hero prefaces each stage of its development by announcing, "Me to play." Precision above all else, even though the

---

[4] Claude Bonnefoy, *Conversations with Eugene Ionesco* (New York, 1971), p. 10.

game he is ending is his own life. It is also a world of such acute self-consciousness that the created characters are continually puncturing the illusion of art: "This," says Clov, "is what is called making an exit"; after a particularly tedious interchange Hamm appropriates the audience's response by remarking, "This is deadly"; Malone writing in bed becomes indistinguishable from Beckett writing in his study, forever breaking off to ensure that the reader is aware that the words he is reading are those that Malone is writing. And so on. When Ionesco is unable to think of an ending, he relapses into whimsy; his characters float away giggling into the heavens, like Babar the Elephant. Beckett's, on the other hand, lapse into arithmetic. *Watt* is particularly prone to this counting mania; page after page is devoted to the possible combinations of notes produced by three frogs croaking "Krak! Krek! Krik!" respectively; to the various ways in which someone might move about a room or dispose of a key; to the family tree of the disastrous Lynches, whose unfulfilled ambition is to achieve a combined age of one thousand years and whose combined ailments would fill a hospital. Similarly, Molloy plots like a computer how to dispose of his sixteen sucking stones in four pockets in such a way that he will never suck the same stone twice in succession. Finally, exacerbated by reason beyond reason, he throws them all away except one, which he promptly loses. Mathematics, as Molloy explains, is the one assured consolation in an unpredictable and literary universe:

> In winter, under my greatcoat, I wrapped myself in swathes of newspaper. . . . The Times Literary Supplement was admirably adapted to this purpose, of a never failing toughness and impermeability. Even farts made no impression on it. I can't help it, gas escapes from my fundament on the least pretext, it's hard not to mention it now and then, however great

my distaste. One day I counted them. Three hundred and fifteen farts in nineteen hours, or an average of over sixteen farts an hour. After all it's not excessive. Four farts every fifteen minutes. It's nothing. Not even one fart every four minutes. It's unbelievable. Damn it, I hardly fart at all, I should never have mentioned it. Extraordinary how mathematics help you to know yourself.

It is a point well and plangently made, although, surprisingly, he has miscalculated: "four farts every fifteen minutes" is more, not less, than "one fart every four minutes." I know of only one other place in Beckett's works where his arithmetic lets him down.[5]

Over the years Beckett's mathematical obsessions have become a little less obtrusive, but they still remain. In an extraordinary late piece of prose, *Imagination Dead Imagine*, the precise positions of two immobile bodies in a sphere are plotted by geometrical coordinates. These bleak notations are all that remain of an experimental program that began around 1930 as a kind of homage to James Joyce and ended as nothing less than the assassination of both the novel and the play in their received, conventional forms.

Of course, Beckett's experiments, like Ionesco's are finally a matter of temperament. Ionesco developed his special form of antitheater because, like many intellectuals, he was contemptuous of the stage. "I started writing for the theater," he once remarked, "because I hated it." Beckett's peculiar revolution seems rooted even deeper. "You would do better," says Molloy, "at least no worse, to obliterate texts than to blacken margins, to fill in the holes of words till all is blank and flat and the whole ghastly business looks like what it is, senseless, speechless, issueless misery." It is as though

---

[5] At the beginning of *Murphy* the hero is described as being lashed naked to his rocking chair by seven scarves; only six are accounted for.

the whole of Beckett's writing career were a search for an adequate artistic expression for his depression and his distaste for art, a slow but inevitable progress from manic high style through obsessionality to the latest minimal works, which are as close to silence as a man can decently get while still remaining a practicing author. He himself summed it up in a 1949 dialogue with Georges Duthuit, when he described the fate of the artist as being resigned to "the expression that there is nothing to express, nothing with which to express, nothing from which to express, no power to express, no desire to express, together with the obligation to express."[6] His career is like the last words of *The Unnamable*: "you must go on, I can't go on, I'll go on."

[6] "Three Dialogues with Georges Duthuit," in *Transition* (1949).

Early Works: A Fairly Strong Young Rose

i

Beckett was born on April 13, 1906, at Foxrock, near Dublin. That year, April 13 was not only a Friday, it was also Good Friday, which seems peculiarly appropriate for a man who subsequently became obsessed both with the Crucifixion and with the sheer ill luck of existence. He first appeared on the literary scene as a relatively conventional member of the highbrow experimental group that surrounded James Joyce in Paris. In many ways he was a natural, for he had much in common with Joyce, both socially and intellectually. Although Beckett writes like someone who has never had a childhood—without nostalgia, regret, vulnerability, or much discernable trace of the more undefended emotions like tenderness—we have the word of his friend, John Calder, that, like Joyce, "Beckett had a comfortable and conventional upbringing in an upper middle-class family that was cultured, liberal and affectionate to an unusual degree."[1] Unlike Joyce, but like many other important Irish writers, Beckett's family was Protestant; he was educated in Ulster at Portora Royal School and went on to Trinity College, Dublin, where he read Modern Languages and eventually took his M.A., an experience which apparently inspired the funniest passage in *Watt*, the oral examination of the research student Louit by Messrs. O'Meldon, Magershon, Fitzwein, de Baker, and MacStern. From 1928 to 1930 he lectured in English at the École Normale Supérieure in Paris, and in French at Trinity College, Dublin, from 1930 to 1932, at which point he abandoned university life, moved for a while to London, wandered around Europe, and finally settled in Paris in 1937.

Beckett joined the Joyce circle in Paris hot from his Dublin M.A.; that is, he seems to have been in the mood to back up his literary ambitions with a good deal of heavy academic muscle. His essay on "Dante . . . Bruno, Vico . . . Joyce," which took opening pride of place in *Our Exagmination*, is a tense, clever but not particularly illuminating act of devotion by a young man with all his learning fresh upon him. Joyce himself was impressed enough by it to say he thought Beckett had promise—a rare gesture for him. In 1930 Beckett proved his devotion by translating part of "Anna Livia Plurabelle" into French, but gave up when he returned to Dublin. Later, Joyce returned the compliment by memorizing passages from Beckett's first novel, *Murphy*.

In those days Beckett appears as an inscrutable figure: a lanky, spectral, silent, and highly intellectual presence, but also—and it seems odd in a man who has immortalized so many hoboes—a particularly sharp

[1] *A Samuel Beckett Reader*, ed. John Calder (London, 1967), p. 8.

dresser. "His clothes," wrote Peggy Guggenheim, "were very French and tight-fitting."[2] Miss Guggenheim confesses that for about eighteen months she was besotted by him, though, from her own account, the passion seems to have been one-sided. Earlier, Joyce's daughter Lucia had felt much the same way, until "Beckett told her bluntly he came to the Joyce flat primarily to see her father."[3] With Joyce himself, Beckett was less ambiguous in his devotion. Although it is not true that he was ever the master's secretary, Joyce did dictate to him one or two bits of *Finnegans Wake*, and certainly the younger man ran errands and dogsbodied fervently enough for someone to have suggested, in all seriousness, that Beckett was his own model for Lucky to Joyce's Pozzo.

The real connection was one of sympathy; not only were their backgrounds and intellectual tastes similar, they were also both martyrs to depression, though in very different ways. Joyce suffered from an older man's depression which grew from a lifetime of private dedication to his own genius and public rejection of it. Beckett's gloom, on the other hand, seems a condition he was born to. That is partly why Beckett, even at his jauntiest, reads like a man who has never had a childhood. Yet depression has also been his constant theme, more or less obscured at first, but emerging more and more powerfully as his age and authority have increased, until he reached that point of despair where he seemed to be writing off his whole life's work. In the middle 1960s he told the Irish novelist Aidan Higgins that words were finished: "Writing style, that vanity, he compared to a bow tie about a throat cancer."[4] It is a desperate statement from one of the most rigorous

[2] *Confessions of an Art Addict* (London, 1960), p. 50.
[3] Richard Ellmann, *James Joyce* (London, 1959), p. 662.
[4] Profile of Aidan Higgins in *The Guardian*, October 11, 1971.

stylists of all time. Yet the seeds of this were present at the start in the long essay on Proust, which Beckett published in 1931, when he was twenty-five. That essay is a clear and curiously prescient expression of most of Beckett's obsessions. It is also stuffed with the aphorisms of despair: "the haze of our smug will to live," "our pernicious and incurable optimism," "the bitterness of fatality," "that desert of loneliness and recrimination that men call love." One sentence sums up the tone: "The suffering of being: that is, the free play of every faculty." In other words, the whole world of feeling and response and attention, which artists like D. H. Lawrence considered the one great good, was for Beckett, even in his early twenties, a guarantee only of suffering. All this might seem merely a young man's modish gloom were it not that everything he has written since has repeated the same message.

According to Richard Ellmann, Joyce found this gloom peculiarly to his taste:

> Beckett was addicted to silences, and so was Joyce; they engaged in conversations which consisted often of silences directed towards each other, both suffused with sadness, Beckett mostly for the world, Joyce mostly for himself. Joyce sat in his habitual posture, legs crossed, toe of the upper leg under the instep of the lower; Beckett, also tall and slender, fell into the same gesture. Joyce suddenly asked some such question as, "How could the idealist Hume write a history?" Beckett replied, "A history of representations." Joyce said nothing. . . .[5]

It sounds like Vladimir and Estragon at their wits' end, although in a comfortable setting and with university educations.

In his relations with Joyce, silence and apathy were the basis of an unexpectedly affectionate cameraderie,

[5] *Op. cit.*, p. 661.

but for Beckett they were also a distinctive personal style. Peggy Guggenheim compared him with Goncharov's Oblomov, with whom he shared the inability to get out of bed in the morning, and the essay on Proust shows that he himself was obsessed by his gloom and lethargy. Although the essay contains some shrewd and original critical insights, *Proust* is, above all, an excuse for Beckett's diagnosis of his own problems. The literary criticism proper, in fact, does not begin until Beckett has allowed himself a long and not altogether relevant disquisition on "the Time cancer" and its attributes, Habit and Memory. According to this, Time is the "poisonous" condition we are born to, constantly changing us without our knowing, finally killing us without our assent. We are doomed to Time because we have committed "the original and eternal sin . . . of having been born," a phrase that re-echoes through the later novels and plays. We expiate that original sin by living, which Beckett considers a peculiarly painful business, and we mitigate the pain of living by Habit, which is another word for Beckett's own apathy:

> Habit is a compromise effected between the individual and his environment, or between the individual and his own organic eccentricities, the guarantee of a dull inviolability, the lightning-conductor of his existence. Habit is the ballast that chains the dog to his vomit. Breathing is habit. Life is habit.

In other words, Habit is an armor protecting us from whatever can be neither predicted nor controlled, from the whole world of feeling which, for Beckett, guarantees only suffering:

> The fundamental duty of Habit . . . consists in a perpetual adjustment and readjustment of our organic sensibility to the conditions of its worlds. Suffering represents the omission of that duty, whether through negligence or inefficiency, and boredom its adequate

performance. The pendulum oscillates between these two terms: Suffering—that opens a window on the real and is the main condition of the artistic experience, and Boredom—with its hosts of tophatted and hygienic ministers, Boredom that must be considered as the most tolerable because the most durable of human evils.

The possibility that life may offer any alternatives to suffering—namely, love or pleasure—simply does not exist. The only consolation is that suffering is a precondition of art; it inspires. Otherwise, the best one can hope for are the infrequent illuminations of "involuntary memory," those associations which flood in unexpectedly to redeem the present with the richness of the past—as when Proust dipped that famous madeleine into his tea. As Beckett describes them, these "immediate and fortuitous act[s] of perception" sound curiously like Joyce's epiphanies. They are, anyway, too intermittent to mitigate the beastly business of living. Their being so undependable has, however, one advantage: it provides a perfect excuse for not writing. It was only much later, above all in *Waiting for Godot*, that Beckett came to terms with his own sensibility and created art out of boredom, not suffering. In this earliest book his message is undifferentiated gloom; he makes it sound as though the noblest human aspiration were to achieve the condition of one of B. F. Skinner's robots, conditioned out of human feeling by boredom.

Yet despite this self-conscious despondency Beckett's writing at this time was, in its polysyllabic way, insistently talkative, almost florid. No doubt Joyce was partly to blame, since his artistic influence on the younger man was overwhelming and certainly for the worse. With one brilliant exception, the short stories Beckett was publishing in avant-garde magazines and collected in 1934 under the title *More Pricks Than Kicks*, were disasters of affectation:

Bodies don't matter but hers went something like this: big enormous breasts, big breech, Botticelli thighs, knock-knees, square ankles, wobbly, poppata, mammose, slobbery-blubbery, bubbubbubbub, a real button-busting Weib, ripe. . . .

This is a parody of Joyce at his most self-parodying, at once preening and secondhand. Beckett was right to refuse to allow the book to be reprinted—except in a limited edition for scholars—until 1970, when it could no longer be held against him. Today, critics wonder at the way in which Beckett's earliest books were unrecognized. It seems to me perfectly understandable. One story apart, the style of *More Pricks* is not that of a natural writer. Instead, it is a pedant's style: a labored grasping at the artificial, combined with a good deal of self-congratulation in the wit.

This is also true of the poems Beckett was writing during his first stay in Paris:

My squinty doaty!
I hid and you sook.
And Francine my precious fruit
    of a house-and-parlour foetus!
What an exfoliation!
Her little grey flayed epidermis
    and scarlet tonsils!
My one child
scourged by a fever to stagnant murky blood. . . .

These lines are from *Whoroscope*, published by Nancy Cunard's Hours Press in 1930. Admittedly, it is a *jeu d'esprit*, written at one night's sitting in order to win a £10 prize Miss Cunard had offered for a poem on Beckett's abiding obsession, Time. Even so, it is miserably like every other experimental production of the period: one hundred lines of text, a large fistful of notes, and an abstruse subject, the private and inner life of Descartes, another of Beckett's old favorites. Its form is that of T. S. Eliot's *The Waste Land*, although it has the dubious distinction of an even higher ratio of notes to text—98 lines and 17 footnotes. Its language—all frenetic punning and muffled Irishism—is Joyce's. The fact that it won the prize makes it no less derivative or affected. With the best will and the most piercing hindsight in the world it would have been impossible to guess that the author was a genius in the making.

Frank Kermode has remarked that Beckett belonged to "the primitivist and decadent *avant garde* of 1932."[6] The special mark of its decadence was, perhaps, that the original fierce and iconoclastic determination to rescue literature from the mindlessness of late romanticism had faded away, leaving only an intellectual dust bowl. Somewhere in *Ulysses* an Oxford don appears pushing a lawn mower that goes "clevercleverclever-clever." It is a good joke, but also prophetic. In *Finnegans Wake* Joyce himself gave in to mere brilliance; he took the fertile experimentalism of the original modernist period, which had seemed to open the arts to areas of experience never properly explored before, and adapted it to the sensibility of a medieval Schoolman. This, it would seem, is why the young Beckett, with all his university pedantry still upon him, found it so alluring.

Beckett was twenty-four when *Whoroscope* was published. Within two years Edward Titus's *This Quarter* printed his story, "Dante and the Lobster," a minor masterpiece which redeems all the excesses of *More Pricks Than Kicks* and is perhaps the best thing Beckett wrote before *Godot.* It has many of the ingredients he was later to use and reuse, beginning with a hero crucified between learning and clownishness. He stars in all the stories in *More Pricks* and is named Belacqua after Dante's prototype of Oblomov, who must redeem a life-

[6] *Modern Essays* (London, 1971), p. 205.

time's sloth on earth by a second lifetime of lethargy, lounging in the shadow of a rock in purgatory. Like Estragon in *Godot*, Belacqua Shuah is tormented by his ruined feet. Like Watt, Molloy, Clov, and the narrator of the three linked stories that begin *No's Knife*, he has a "spavined gait." To be unable, or unwilling, to bend their legs at the knees is a mark of distinction for Beckett's heroes; Watt is the most extreme: each step twists him galvanically through at least ninety degrees, like a primitive puppet, in what Beckett calls "a head-long tardigrade." Perhaps it is an outward and visible sign of their inward and spiritual collapse. Certainly, Belacqua's jerky and grotesque appearance matches his inner life, which is continually erupting into impotent fierceness only to sink back appalled. His fierceness is impotent because it is the fierceness of the self with the clogging ineptitude of the body. This is no longer a problem for the later heroes: bedridden, stuffed in urns, sunk in mud or sand, they are beyond their bodies. But Belacqua, like his creator at that time, was "a fairly strong young rose" who can still find satisfaction in a little excess, like his successor in the Beckett canon, Murphy, whose pleasure it is to lash himself naked to a rocking chair and then rock and rock into nirvana.

The plot of "Dante and the Lobster" is straightforward, a simple day in the life of Belacqua Shuah as he ponders a problem from Dante; obsessionally prepares a fiery lunch of carbonized toast, salt, mustard, cayenne, and Gorgonzola; visits a fishmonger to collect a lobster for his aunt; has an Italian lesson where he and his weary teacher discuss, in a desultory way, Dante's views on pity and damnation. Meanwhile, the lobster, waiting in the hall outside, is attacked by a cat. It is elegant, witty, but not otherwise out of the ordinary until the final scene draws all the threads together:

Belacqua drew near to the house of his aunt. Let us call it Winter, that dusk may fall now and a moon rise. At the corner of the street a horse was down and a man sat on its head. I know, thought Belacqua, that that is considered the right thing to do. But why? A lamplighter flew by on his bike, tilting with his pole at the standards, jousting a little yellow light into the evening. A poorly dressed couple stood in the bay of a pretentious gateway, she sagging against the railings, her head lowered, he standing facing her. He stood up close to her, his hands dangling by his sides. Where we were, thought Belacqua, as we were. He walked on, gripping his parcel. Why not piety and pity both, even down below? Why not mercy and Godliness together? A little mercy in the stress of sacrifice, a little mercy to rejoice against judgment. He thought of Jonah and the gourd and the pity of a jealous God on Nineveh. And poor McCabe, he would get it in the neck at dawn. What was he doing now, how was he feeling? He would relish one more meal, one more night.

His aunt was in the garden, tending whatever flowers die at that time of year. She embraced him and together they went down into the bowels of the earth, into the kitchen in the basement. She took the parcel and undid it and abruptly the lobster was on the table, on the oilcloth, discovered.

"They assured me it was fresh" said Belacqua.

Suddenly he saw the creature move, this neuter creature. Definitely it changed its position. His hand flew to his mouth.

"Christ!" he said "it's alive."

His aunt looked at the lobster. It moved again. It made a faint nervous act of life on the oilcloth. They stood above it, looking down on it, exposed cruciform on the oilcloth. It shuddered again. Belacqua felt he would be sick.

"My God" he whined "it's alive, what'll we do?"

The aunt simply had to laugh. She bustled off to the pantry to fetch her smart apron, leaving him goggling down at the lobster, and came back with it on and her sleeves rolled up, all business.

"Well" she said "it is to be hoped so, indeed."

"All this time" muttered Belacqua. Then, suddenly aware of her hideous equipment: "What are you going to do?" he cried.

"Boil the beast" she said, "what else?"

"But it's not dead" protested Belacqua "you can't boil it like that."

She looked at him in astonishment. Had he taken leave of his senses?

"Have sense" she said sharply, "lobsters are always boiled alive. They must be." She caught up the lobster and laid it on its back. It trembled. "They feel nothing" she said.

In the depths of the sea it had crept into the cruel pot. For hours, in the midst of its enemies, it had breathed secretly. It had survived the Frenchwoman's cat and his witless clutch. Now it was going alive into scalding water. It had to. Take into the air my quiet breath.

Belacqua looked at the old parchment of her face, grey in the dim kitchen.

"You make a fuss" she said angrily "and upset me and then lash into it for your dinner."

She lifted the lobster clear of the table. It had about thirty seconds to live.

Well, thought Belacqua, it's a quick death, God help us all.

It is not.

A cabby sitting on his horse's head, a couple of desolate lovers, a moment's vague attention to the theological question of God's dubious mercy, a thought for the condemned murderer McCabe: these are urban horrors, casual and scarcely noticed, mere preludes to the melancholy aunt, "tending whatever flowers die at that time of the year," who descends with Belacqua, like Virgil with Dante, "into the bowels of the earth." And suddenly the abstract questions of suffering and mercy are made explicit in that least human of living creatures, the lobster, "exposed cruciform on the oilcloth." Even Keats, musing on his own death in the "Ode to a Nightingale," seems perfectly appropriate to "this neuter creature's" agony: "Take into the air my quiet breath." A mild, bookish day with Dante ends with a real, though infinitely small scale vision of hell.

It is a passage of extraordinary power and stripped eloquence that seems to forecast everything that was later to preoccupy Beckett and much that he was later to achieve. There is, for example, that anguish so piercing that it must be displaced before it can be expressed. So Moran, the proto-Pozzo in *Molloy*, treats his son like a dog but grieves like a lover for his dead hens. So Malone, usually bored and tight-lipped in the stories he tells to while away the time it takes to die, has an uncharacteristically plangent passage about killing small animals in his tale of the abused child Sapo, for whom he otherwise spares no pity. Perhaps the whole starved and tattered cast of clowns, tramps, and cripples who fill Beckett's works are as near ordinary humanity as the author will allow himself, lobsters by any other name. They allow him to displace pity into their vaudeville misfortunes. Beckett's method as an artist is like the mechanism of dreams, where the real agonies are expressed only by displacement and disguise. Without that displacement the dreamer would wake, the author be thrust undefended into that Proustian world of feeling which, he says, guarantees only suffering.

There is, however, nothing sidelong about the story's end:

Well, thought Belacqua, it's a quick death, God help us all.
It is not.

That voice out of nowhere is speaking for all Beckett's subsequent heroes, summing up in three words all that they have to say: Watt gently muttering his story to a friend in a madhouse, Molloy and Malone in their beds endlessly writing until death comes to relieve them, the Unnamable apparently beyond life yet unable to die, the narrator of *How It Is* sunk in the mud in his half-world, the two immobile but still faintly breathing figures cramped in their harshly lit sphere in *Imagination Dead Imagine*, The Lost Ones shuffling and searching, Hamm finally alone and still under his blood-stained handkerchief, Winnie in *Happy Days* jauntily prattling on while the sand rises toward her mouth, the three characters in *Play* perpetually repeating the ritual of their jealousy, Krapp listening to his past on tape, and, above all, Estragon yearning for death in a warm, dry climate where "they crucify quick." All of them in their different ways, while they endure the muffled agonies of Habit and Boredom, repeat those three words, "It is not."

All this is hindsight. But there is also a simpler point to make. "Dante and the Lobster" was published within a couple of years of *Whoroscope*, that monument of stuck-up intellectuality, when Beckett was only twenty-six. Yet the story already has most of the marks of his genius: the concentration and absolutely controlled simplicity of language, the easy movement between the colloquial and the allusive, the interplay between wit, compassion, and despair, and the final shocked affirmation of pain. In other words, Beckett's prose—in this story at least—already had the subtle tautness usually associated with poetry, while his verse— a handful of later and mostly French lyrics apart— fritters itself away in postures and imitation. From these early and mostly unpromising beginnings the progress of his work was one of a gradual chastening of style, stripping away artifice in order to achieve a final bleak meticulousness; that is, the progress of his work has been undeviatingly toward the condition of poetry. But he has achieved this—in his novels, plays, and works for radio—only in prose.

The Novels: Desolation Row

After Beckett gave up university teaching in 1932 he spent five years more or less footloose, in London and around the Continent, before he finally settled in Paris in 1937. Hugh Kenner has described him during this period as "a wandering scholar," which fits neatly the finicky precision, sourness, and medieval pedantry, that mixture of self-denigration and conceit which marks much of his early style.

The result of this haphazard pilgrimage was a not particularly distinguished volume of poems, *Echo's Bones*, 1935, and his first novel, *Murphy*, published unnoticed in 1938. Although the novel is a stage further on from *More Pricks Than Kicks*, without the more hectic Joycean puns and affectations which made most of the short

stories so hard to love or even read, it still belongs to
the same world. The setting is London, but the book has
a full cast of Dublin monsters, all constellated around
the hero for their own seedy sexual or financial ends.
Like Belacqua Shuah, like Beckett himself, Murphy has
most of the characteristics of the malcontent wandering
scholar: he is stricken with poverty and idleness, exacerbated, misanthropic, overeducated to the point of
despair. The dog's life he leads is redeemed only by the
pleasures of the mind. He is, in fact, a solipsist who
pictures his mind as a "hollow sphere" containing
everything, like the skull-like room with its two high
eye-windows in which *Endgame* is played. When Murphy
eventually finds his terrestrial bower of bliss it turns out
to be a padded cell; like the inside of his skull, it is
oyster gray. Before that, his only way through to
mental peace had been by devoutly rocking while bound
naked to a chair. He eventually dies rocking and happy:
someone pulls the wrong chain in the lavatory; this
turns on the gas in Murphy's bedroom, which is promptly
ignited by his lit candle; Murphy, lashed tight to his
rocking chair, burns to death. "A classical case of
misadventure," says the coroner.

As in life, so in death. A will is discovered asking
that his body be cremated and his ashes flushed down
the toilet in the Abbey Theatre, preferably during a
performance. The man entrusted with this solemn duty
gets drunk and hurls the bag of ashes at a fellow
boozer in a pub:

> By closing time the body, mind and soul of Murphy
> were freely distributed over the floor of the saloon;
> and before another dayspring greyened the earth had
> been swept away with the sand, the beer, the butts,
> the glass, the matches, the spits, the vomit.

There is a certain beady-eyed slapstick about all this,
as though Beckett were anxious not to be caught taking

his hero, or anything else except his elegant style, too seriously. All Murphy's grand philosophical aspirations come down to this in the end: not even ash on an old man's sleeve, just ash on a barroom floor. The only person who is allowed to grieve for Murphy's passing is Celia, his dumb but devoted mistress, who is by profession a prostitute. The book ends with her tentatively mourning, but once again back on the job. Apart from Murphy, she is the only real character in the book, although only vaguely and passively so, since she is overborne by her condition and her abuse. The other figures are as two-dimensional as Ben Jonson's humours; they talk stylishly in the Dublin barroom-academical manner, but are manipulated galvanically, like puppets.

For the purposes of the novel this flatness is all Beckett needs, since what he is writing is, above all, a comedy of manners and high style. On that level, *Murphy* is a considerable advance on *More Pricks*, in which the jokes were so encrusted with mannerism as to be scarcely recognizable. In *Murphy*, Beckett allows his humor more elbowroom and gains, as a result, more clarity:

> He sat up and found himself at the feet of a low-sized corpulent middle-aged woman with very bad duck's disease indeed.
> Duck's disease is a distressing pathological condition in which the thighs are suppressed and the buttocks spring directly from behind the knees, aptly described in Steiss's nosonomy as Panpygoptosis. Happily its incidence is small and confined, as the popular name suggests, to the weaker vessel, a bias of Nature bitterly lamented by the celebrated Dr. Busby and other less pedantic notables. It is non-contagious (though some observers have held the contrary), non-infectious, non-heritable, painless and intractable. Its aetiology remains obscure to all but

the psychopathological wholehogs, who have shown it to be simply another embodiment of the neurotic *Non me rebus sed mihi res.*

The Duck, to give her a name to go on with, held in one hand a large bulging bag and in the other a lead whereby her personality was extended to a Dachshund so low and so long that Murphy had no means of telling whether it was a dog or a bitch, which was the first thing he wanted to know about every so-called dog that came before him. It certainly had the classical bitch's eye, kiss me in the cornea, keep me in the iris and God help you in the pupil. But some dogs had that.

In his earliest days Beckett's demented scholarship had been a matter of pride; now it is a source of enjoyment and it works for him. He uses it as though it were funny in itself, not just a mark of his allegiance to the Joyce faction of the *avant-garde.* The result is a slow-motion ballet of absurd learning, continually teetering on the edge of slapstick and then miraculously recovering. (Given Beckett's obsession with detail, the references may all be genuine, although "Panpygoptosis" is beyond even the largest Oxford dictionary.)

In its ornate way, *Murphy* has its own special perfection and contains not one ill-written sentence. Each phrase seems brooded upon, composed infinitely slowly with a fine ear, sensitive as a bat's, for its faintest reverberations. So, too, with the book's structure: the plot notches into place like a jigsaw puzzle; by the last page every detail has been taken up and given its own special twist. The result is a formal perfection that even Flaubert might have been proud of. Beckett would never again make obeisance toward these nineteenth-century virtues in his novels. Yet in some way the perfections cut the book off, making it seem in the end oddly miniature, like some exquisite Fabergé egg, the product of endless care and skill and discipline, but tiny and self-enclosed. Camus once spoke of the creator who makes "the air echo with the sterile secret he possesses." In *Murphy* the secret is, precisely, sterile: nothing moves, nothing is renewed, nothing seems possible after it. It is his first novel; it might easily have been his last.

Yet at the center of the book is a perception Beckett was later to use and reuse, although in very different ways. Murphy, browbeaten into finding a job by Celia, becomes a male nurse in a lunatic asylum, the Magdalen Mental Mercyseat. And wholly to his surprise, work, which as a member of the drinking class he had naturally looked on as a curse, becomes a vocation, an illumination, the source of what Joyce would have called an epiphany. It is, in short, love at first sight between him and the patients, immediate, dramatic, irrevocable:

> They caused Murphy no horror. The most easily identifiable of his immediate feelings were respect and unworthiness. Except for the manic . . . the impression he received was of that self-immersed indifference to the contingencies of the contingent world which he had chosen for himself as the only felicity and achieved so seldom.

This seems natural enough considering that Murphy's most persistent ambition was to cut himself adrift from his unsatisfactory body and float off into the silent inner world of the mind. Moreover, his way of doing this was by endlessly rocking, like an autistic child. What is surprising is the completeness of his revelation, its power of making sense of all those confusions which had previously seemed unresolvable:

> The patients were described as "cut off" from reality, from the rudimentary blessings of the layman's reality, if not altogether, as in the severer cases, then in certain fundamental respects. The function of treatment was to bridge the gulf, to translate the sufferer from

his own pernicious little private dungheap to the glorious world of discrete particles, where it would be his inestimable prerogative once again to wonder, love, hate, desire, rejoice and howl in a reasonable balanced manner, and comfort himself with the society of others in the same predicament.

All this was duly revolting to Murphy, whose experience as a physical and rational being obliged him to call sanctuary what the psychiatrists called exile and to think of the patients not as banished from a system of benefits but as escaped from a colossal fiasco. . . .

The issue therefore, as lovingly simplified and perverted by Murphy, lay between nothing less fundamental than the big world and the little world, decided by the patients in favour of the latter, revived by the psychiatrists on behalf of the former, in his own case unresolved. In fact, it was unresolved, only in fact. His vote was cast. "I am not of the big world, I am of the little world" was an old refrain with Murphy.

In the 1970s it has become a fashionable cant to believe that the schizophrenic in his madness is somehow closer to the truth than the rest of us in our so-called sanity. But not in 1938. It may even have been read as a joke at Murphy's expense that a man so learned and so besotted with abstraction could find happiness only in the company of the insane. But at another level Beckett clearly was not joking. He means what he says about the power and fascination of schizophrenia, though his particular version of it is controlled, illuminated, and transformed into art in a way R. D. Laing's wilder cohorts would hardly admire. To put it another way, the pausing, dandified prose of *Murphy* owes a great deal to Joyce and the decadent modernist style which survived in Paris into the 1930s, but the insight Beckett was working toward—or which he had had far earlier but was only now beginning to express in his work—belongs to a much later period. In other words, *Murphy* is his first step toward creating a powerful and perfect artistic world out of those states of mind which were once denied and hidden away in lunatic asylums but which, by the 1960s, had come to seem mirror images of our own world.

This becomes clear when Murphy discovers his soulmate and Narcissus image, Mr. Endon, a tiny, hairy, elegantly pajamaed and beringed schizophrenic with whom he plays day-long, silent, unfinished games of chess, which both of them try to lose:

> Mr. Endon was a schizophrenic of the most amiable variety, at least for the purposes of such a humble and envious outsider as Murphy. The languor in which he passed his days, while deepening every now and then to the extent of some charming suspension of gesture, was never so profound as to inhibit all movement. His inner voice did not harangue him, it was unobtrusive and melodious, a gentle continuo in the whole consort of his hallucinations. The bizarreri of his attitudes never exceeded a stress laid on their grace. In short, a psychosis so limpid and imperturbable that Murphy felt drawn to it as Narcissus to his fountain.

Mr. Endon's gentle, silent dottiness sounds like Watt's; his inner voices are like those heard, almost without exception, by all of Beckett's later heroes, from Watt and Molloy to Winnie, Joe, and the narrator of *How It Is*, with his ritually repeated "I say it as I hear it." As for "the languor in which he passed his days," Miss Guggenheim compared Beckett at that period to Oblomov, and the author himself named his first hero after Dante's Belacqua. In short, Mr. Endon is a real Narcissus image: Murphy's—and perhaps Beckett's—life end on.

At this stage of his development, however, Beckett cannot yet use the theme for what it really is. The

Joycean elegance of his language gets in his way; he cannot shed the need to be clever and allusive. His style is like the rather heavy farce by which Murphy's ambitions, illuminations, and death are made finally ridiculous. Both look like manic defenses against the depression that permeates the novel and the unblinkingly pessimistic vision of sanity and madness on which it centers.

WATT

There is a remarkable logic and inevitability about Beckett's progress. The same themes reappear from work to work, each time extended a little further, a little deeper. So, too, with the heroes; it is as though their creator were always just one step ahead of them. If Murphy had written instead of rocked, he would probably have written like the author of the Belacqua stories. Watt, in his turn, is a stage beyond Murphy. Whereas Murphy idealized the schizophrenics from the outside, Watt is one. He tells his story to a man called Sam, like Beckett himself, who is a fellow inmate of a lunatic asylum much like the Magdalen Mental Mercyseat. What he tells and how he tells it are, in their different ways, symptoms of his condition.

The story itself is simple enough. Watt, a gentle, abused, and bemused figure, who moves like a broken doll and dresses like a tramp, arrives at the house of Mr. Knott, where he is to replace a servant called Arsène. On his way there he suffers various minor indignities: he first appears ejected angrily from a tram; a railway porter wheeling a milk churn knocks him over; an eccentric aristocrat called Lady McCann throws a stone at him; he takes a rest by rolling unhesitatingly into a ditch. Arrived finally at Mr. Knott's, he submits to a long harangue from the departing

Arsène, then silently and unquestioningly assumes the duties of ground-floor servant, attending to the rituals of the Knott household, which are as elaborate and formalized as those of a Pharaoh. In due course he graduates to the upper floor and the rituals of the bedroom, where he takes the place of Erskine, the senior servant whose time is now up. Finally, his cycle completed, he leaves as silently as he came. When last seen at the railway station he is being abused as usual: the stationmaster knocks him flat and injures him by violently flinging open a door; a bucket of slimy water is emptied over him. But he rises without comment or complaint, mildly requests a ticket to the end of the line, and mildly fades away. It is a beautiful summer morning; all present agree that, for once, it is almost good to be alive. But the reader already knows that Watt's next stop is the lunatic asylum, since the chronological end has already come in the third of the book's four parts, when Watt disappears from the narrator walking backward, "over the deep threshing shadows backwards stumbling," having gradually inverted his whole life; he not only moves backwards, his sentence structure, word order, finally the order of the letters in the words have also been turned back to front. His world has become, literally, end on.

As for Mr. Knott: as his name implies, he is like Godot, an unseen but powerful presence, or rather absence—mysterious, wealthy, but unpredictable—who controls every detail of his servants' lives yet is only glimpsed momentarily brooding in his garden, like God in Eden. The rest, as in any religion, is ritual and mystery.

"No symbols where none intended," reads the last of the novel's witty addenda. I think we should take the author's word for this, despite a mass of interpretations to the contrary. For what emerges most powerfully from the novel is not any stunning allegory of, say, the nature of the Godhead—who resembles Mr. Knott in being defined only by negations, just as Watt, when his madness is most upon him, is said to look like Bosch's Christ. Instead, the subject is total obsession. In other words, the book is a work of extreme mannerism, a mannerism deliberately pushed to the point of lunacy.

To put it stylistically, the overwriting which virtually scuppered all but one of the stories in *More Pricks* was refined in *Murphy* into a tone of elegant pedantry, cadenced, polysyllabic, and shimmering with learned, although mostly bogus, references. In short, the mannerism in *More Pricks* was a vice; in *Murphy* it was part of the wit. But in *Watt* it flowers into full-blown psychosis. It is a question both of what Beckett says and of how he says it. For example, the movement of the prose is so hesitant, so riddled with commas, that it virtually ceases to move at all:

> But if Watt's mouth was open, and his jaw sunk, and his eyes glassy, and his head sunk, and his knees bent, and his back bent, his mind was busy, busy wondering which was best, to shut the door, from which he felt the draught, on the nape, of his neck, and set down his bags, and sit down, or to shut the door, and set down his bags, without sitting down, or to shut the door, and sit down, without setting down his bags, or to set down his bags, and sit down, without shutting the door, or to shut the door, from which he felt the blast, on the nape, of his neck, without setting down his bags, or sitting down, or to set down his bags, without bothering to shut the door, or sit down, or to sit down, without troubling to set down his bags, or shut the door, or to leave things as they were, the bags pulling at his hands, the floor pushing at his feet, and the air puffing, through the door, on the nape, of his neck. . . .

There are 250 pages of this pausing, devious, repetitive withdrawal from statement, 250 pages of qualification after qualification, a hesitant, slightly hiccuping timidity masquerading as precision. It is like a squirrel running round his treadmill: there is an enormous expenditure of prose in order to say more or less nothing and go more or less nowhere, an expense of spirit in a waste of mannerism.

In effect, this getting nowhere is the whole point of the style. What happens to Watt is unimportant since, after all, hardly anything does happen to him. Even so, Watt defends himself against the few vague events that do impinge on him by the most rigorous obsessionality. When we first meet him, he is failing to listen to some passing bore because, like Mr. Endon, he has his inner voices to attend to: "But Watt heard nothing of this, because of other voices, singing, crying, stating, murmuring, things unintelligible, in his ear." Thereafter those inner voices are not mentioned. Instead, they are replaced by an even crazier habit of mind: each detail of life in Mr. Knott's mercifully tranquil household is methodically brooded upon, logically analyzed and reanalyzed so that no possible explanation can be missed. His food, for example:

To whom, Watt wondered, was this arrangement due? To Mr. Knott himself? Or to some other person, to a past domestic perhaps of genius for example, or a professional dietician? And if not to Mr. Knott himself, but to some other person (or of course persons), did Mr. Knott know that such an arrangement existed, or did he not? . . .

Twelve possibilities occurred to Watt, in this connection:

1. Mr. Knott was responsible for the arrangement, and knew that he was responsible for the arrangement, and knew that such an arrangement existed, and was content.

2. Mr. Knott was not responsible for the arrangement, but knew who was responsible for the arrange-

ment, and knew that such an arrangement existed, and was content. . . .

12. Mr. Knott was not responsible for the arrangement, but knew that he was responsible for the arrangement, but did not know that any such arrangement existed, and was content.

This is probably meant to be funny, and in a couple of instances I have already mentioned it is genuinely so: the history of the catastrophic Lynch family and the oral examination of the graduate student Louit. It is also undoubtedly supposed to describe Watt's gently logic-chopping, slow-motion habit of mind: "To explain had always been to exorcize, for Watt." But why this overriding need to exorcize, and is it the inner or outer world that is being exorcized?

Hugh Kenner excuses the style as deliberate witty pedantry and traces it back to Beckett's continual interest in Descartes and an obscure follower called Arnold Geulincx, an Occasionalist. This is interesting and may even be true, but it does not explain why a style that begins as a more or less charming eccentricity so swiftly degenerates into real madness. What is certain is that Watt would have needed to show no further symptoms to justify his confinement in the lunatic asylum where he ends. He reacts to the mild occasions of his life like someone whose inner world is so terrifying that to contain it he must account in advance for every possible eventuality, like a man who can keep out his demons only by blocking every tiny chink in the floorboards. This is obsessional thinking on the far edge of madness. More simply, Watt's demented pondering is a defense against the dangerous unpredictability of life which Beckett had eloquently denounced in *Proust* as a guarantee only of suffering. It is Habit and Boredom raised to the power of psychosis. It is also a state of mind Beckett himself seems to have found fascinating or congenial, for most of his later heroes, particularly in the novels, suffer from it.

It may be that Beckett adopted this style with the highest artistic intentions, for its possible wit and the illumination it sheds on Watt's mentality. But its final effect is deadening. I suggested that one of Joyce's weirder achievements was to adapt the modernist style to the sensibility of a medieval Schoolman. Beckett took that tendency one decisive stage further. Had Duns Scotus been alive and well and writing novels in the twentieth century, he might have written *Watt*. It is as though Beckett wanted to show that questions like how many angels can dance on the head of a pin, or how many dog's dinners can be gleaned from Mr. Knott's leftovers, are still so absorbing that a whole novel can be made out of them. Yet apart from the opening pages of *Watt*, which sound very like *Ulysses*, Joyce's influence is less noticeable than it had been in the earlier work. What the two writers have in common at this stage is a mannerist vice. With Joyce this takes the form of aesthetic arrogance, a belief that his genius was so supreme that its every whim was justified, since the ideal reader would devote a lifetime to decoding *Finnegans Wake*. Beckett's personal style is the reverse of Joyce's; it is that of the hermit crab, passive, defended, unmoving. But perhaps Joyce's devotion to his own obscurity made it easier for Beckett to retire into the shell of his own vices, his verbal and stylistic self-indulgence, his overpowering obsessionality. Between them they were attempting to take the art form of the novel and wring its neck.

The perverse self-destructiveness of Beckett's effort is obvious. Faced with page after page of minute logical alternatives, the reader, however admiring or determined, can in the end only skip. The narrator speaks of incidents "of great formal brilliance and indeterminable purport." In the final analysis the purport is so pigheadedly indeterminable that the formality begins to seem less brilliant than merely tiresome and wanton. Perhaps this is always a risk in any book about a madman living at the center of his madness. The difficulty with *Watt* is that the essence of the hero's madness—however bemused, gentle, and occasionally funny he may be—is a genius for boredom, which the younger Beckett had already gone on record as believing to be a saving grace. In the end, the book is genuinely unreadable and, as it proved, unpublishable. It had to wait ten years to be printed, by which time *Godot* had appeared and Beckett was already famous.

CHANGE OF LANGUAGE, CHANGE OF LIFE

Strangely enough, *Watt* was written during the one period when Beckett was living a life of action and some danger—however unwillingly and in however idiosyncratic a way. It is hard to be precise with such a deliberately shadowy figure, but the facts, as reported by Hugh Kenner and other scholars, are fairly clear. When war broke out in 1939 Beckett was in Ireland, visiting his mother. "I immediately returned to France," he told Kenner. "I preferred France in war to Ireland in peace. I just made it in time."[1] Better, apparently, the German devil he did not know than the Irish one he did. But it was a touchy decision, even for an unpolitical person holding a neutral passport. During the first two years of the Nazi occupation of France, Beckett devoted himself to the apparently neutral task of translating *Murphy* into French; given the allusive and finicky quality of the prose, it was a project only marginally less demanding than the translation of *Finnegans Wake* he had begun ten years before. But he

[1] Hugh Kenner, *Samuel Beckett* (London, 1962), p. 21.

was also involved in less abstract affairs: he was working for the Resistance with his old friend Alfred Péron, whom he had first met at the École Normale Supérieure in 1928. Péron was finally arrested by the Germans and never reappeared;[2] Beckett himself left his apartment one step ahead of the Gestapo. He hid for six weeks in Paris and then escaped to the Vaucluse in Vichy France. There, at Roussillon, from 1942 to 1944, he wrote *Watt*, finishing it in Dublin in 1945. The abstraction and mild dottiness of that book become stranger and more compelling when seen as a means of escape from his own menaced situation; so do the intimations of psychosis which give the work its never quite suppressed ground bass of threat and disaster.

Watt was clearly a dead end, however. That way madness lay, both literally and stylistically. Moreover, by the time the war ended and *Watt* was finished, Beckett was almost forty, too old for mannerism, too old for intellectual affectations, certainly too old to be still under the influence of another writer. He was into that dark period of what Elliott Jacques has called "the mid-life crisis,"[3] when earlier achievement no longer seems enough and, in order to go on at all, it is necessary to change radically. In 1945 Beckett went back to Ireland for a month in order to see his mother. "Then," writes Kenner, "homeless still, he made his way through Normandy back to Paris, reclaimed his old flat, and commenced the siege in the room that was to last until 1950."[4]

It was a period of extraordinary creativity. In his first sixteen years as a writer Beckett had written two novels, a book of stories, a pamphlet of criticism,

[2] He died a few days after being liberated from Mauthausen concentration camp.
[3] Elliott Jacques, "Death and the Mid-Life Crisis," *International Journal of Psycho-Analysis* 46 (1965), 502–514.
[4] Kenner, *op. cit.*, p. 24.

some poems, and a handful of reviews. Now, in less than six years, he turned out four novels—*Molloy, Malone Dies, The Unnamable,* and *Mercier et Camier,* an over-elegant essay in high style and Godotesque dialogue which he suppressed until 1970; two plays—*Waiting for Godot* and *Eleuthéria,* which he has never allowed out; and three stories at the beginning of *No's Knife.* This surge of productivity ended in 1950, when his mother died; for about two years he struggled with the aptly titled *Texts for Nothing* and then was silent, although *Godot* brought him international fame. Then in 1956 there was another, less concentrated burst which lasted until 1962, during which period he produced roughly a work a year: *Endgame, All That Fall, Krapp's Last Tape, Embers, How It Is, Happy Days,* and *Play.* But by that time he was simply extending a worldwide reputation established by that first long and infinitely laborious vigil when he shed the name, style, and indolent habits of his early hero Belacqua and transformed himself into a productive and absolutely original master.

It was a radical change and Beckett accomplished it by radical means: everything he wrote between 1945 and 1950 was written not in English, but in French. No doubt this seemed perfectly natural after all the years he had spent in France and the wartime troubles he had seen there. But just as his decision to return to France in 1939 turned out to be a genuine existential choice, committing him to dangers that were hardly his style, so his decision to write in French proved equally crucial; it was, at last, a final break with his past. This was not simply a matter of getting out from under Joyce's shadow; *Watt* had more or less done that for him, and anyway Joyce had died in 1941, leaving his followers in that most final of all dead ends, *Finnegans Wake,* which is scarcely more fertile an influence than the *Oxford English Dictionary.* To write in French meant escaping from the whole weight of the

Irish rhetoric Beckett had been born to, with its insidious cadences and genius for baroque linguistic flourish. "In the beginning was the pun," says Murphy, prototype Irish stylist and intellectual. In his day Beckett had produced his fair share of Irish high style. But in temperament, as the Proust essay had shown at the start, he was too austere and pessimistic to be satisfied with such ornate gratifications. He needed a medium at once more neutral and more precise. To that end French was the perfect instrument, because it is a language that does not lend itself easily to punning; its own special rhetoric runs continually toward abstraction. This was exactly what Beckett required as he completed his break with the traditional novel and shifted into those plotless, placeless monologues, delivered in a monotone in some no man's land of the spirit. The precise locations of the earlier novels—Belacqua Shuah's Dublin, Murphy's West London, Mr. Knott's house within commuting distance of Dublin, like Foxrock where Beckett was born—gradually dissolve away, first into the vague geography of *Molloy*, with its town, plain, seaside, and forest, none of which is ever quite brought into focus, then shrinking through successive stages of immobility and claustrophobia: Malone bedridden with a view of the house opposite, the Unnamable encased in an urn in some kind of purgatory, the narrator of *How It Is* faintly stirring in an afterworld of mud. The heroes in their turn become more and more disembodied and uncharacterized, losing habits, memories, even limbs, until they become simply unnamable and unnamed. It was most likely easier to achieve this despairing degree of abstraction in a language other than English which, despite every experiment, remains stubbornly specific, thick with local associations and echoes of other voices. In comparison, French seems a model of clarity and logic, and Beckett has used it in such a pure and translucent way that his

French works lose nothing by being translated into the English he was born to. Admittedly, Beckett himself has done the translations, and, among his many gifts, he is a translator of genius. Yet the fact remains, he has evolved a style that is clear, hard, precise, and yet as without history and associations as the characters who speak it.

Beckett's move into French is also part of that spirit of negation he has so persistently explored. It involves a cat's cradle of complications which Watt might have been proud of: an Irishman living in Paris, writing in French about Irishmen, then translating himself triumphantly back into English. And he genuinely transformed himself in the process: through his translations from his own French he has emerged as a master of English prose, which he certainly was not when he wrote only in English. In other words, even his creativity begins with a refusal, a denial of everything he had been up until that moment at the beginning of middle age when he began to write in a foreign language.

It could hardly have been otherwise, for the final, irreducible content of all Beckett's work is depression: " 'It's a quick death, God help us all.' It is not." In the earlier books, that depression had been disguised by wit and pedantry, by Bohemian oddity and manic flourishes of high style. Perhaps that combination of despair and mannerism had been one of the reasons why Beckett had written so slowly, so apparently unwillingly, and why he had complained so plangently to Georges Duthuit of his fate as an artist: "The expression that there is nothing to express, nothing with which to express, nothing from which to express, no power to express, no desire to express, together with the obligation to express." Beckett's dialogues with Duthuit were published in 1949, so presumably they took place while he was at work on his trilogy, *Molloy*, *Malone Dies*, and *The Unnamable*. His predicament is clear at last because he has decided not only to face it directly but also to use it as a source of inspiration.

According to Elliott Jacques, the mid-life crisis is a long period of turmoil and depression, a genuine dark night of the soul, precipitated by the obscure realization that one is really going to die and that the irreversible processes of decay have already begun. Unlike most people, Beckett does not seem to have arrived at that insight in middle age. On the contrary, he has the air of a man born with the taste of death in his mouth. However comfortable and loving his middle-class background may have been, his inner world seems always to have been as deprived and grieving and desolate as that of an Auschwitz child. As a result, his particular resolution of the mid-life crisis was different from that of most other artists. The late works of Beethoven and Shakespeare, for example, are more profound, reflective, ultimately more serene than anything they had achieved before, as though their acceptance of age and mortality had released them into a new, richer dimension of feeling. In comparison, Beckett's work does not change in essence or even in theme; it simply becomes purer, starker, less deviating. The distractions drop away— both the formal distractions of mannerism and even plot, and the personal distractions of sloth and Bohemian oddity—leaving only a solitary man staring beadily and with distaste into the heart of his depression; staring, that is, at his own death-in-life. His writing becomes a way not of avoiding death but of achieving it:

All this business of a labour to accomplish, before I can end, of words to say, a truth to recover, in order to say it, before I can end, of an imposed task, once known, long neglected, finally forgotten, to perform, before I can be done with speaking, done with listening, I invented it all, in the hope it would console me, help me to go on, allow me to think of myself as somewhere on a road, moving, between a beginning and an end, gaining ground, losing ground, getting lost, but somehow in the long run making headway. All lies. I have nothing to do, that is to say nothing in particular. I have to speak, whatever that means. Having nothing to say, no words but the words of others, I have to speak. No one compels me to, there is no one, it's an accident, a fact. Nothing can ever exempt me from it. . . .

This is the Unnamable droning sourly on in his special purgatory. He sounds much like Molloy composing his "long sonata of the dead" or Malone yearning for the moon: "To be dead, before her, on her, with her, and turn, dead on dead, about poor mankind, and never have to die any more, from among the living." The key to the trilogy and to everything that has followed it is in that combination of weariness and doggedness, the desire to die and the senseless need to go on.

In 1945 Beckett made an existential choice more important than the decision that had brought him back to France or turned him to the French language. It was the decision simply to have done with his old wandering and distracted indolence and, instead, to sit down at his table and write, daily, unremittingly, until he had said his desolate say. As it turned out, he remained in his room for almost six years, which in the circumstances was a heroic eternity. This was not merely a major creative effort, but also a major effort of the will and self-definition. Perhaps this was no more, no less than any other serious artist yoking memory and imagination together to produce order among the confusions of experience. But with Beckett the attempt seems starker, less disguised. Throughout the trilogy the narrators' voices are more important than their narrations, increasingly so since the plot disappears altogether as the work progresses. Increasingly, too, the distinctions between the narrators and Beckett himself are eroded: most of the characters from Beckett's previous fiction reappear in the trilogy with one narrator or another claiming credit for them; similarly, whatever name he happens to be using at the time, the voice is Beckett's: Molloy writing in bed in his mother's room, Moran writing through the night, Malone in another bed in another room, the Unnamable limbless in his urn yet writing by some mysterious process he never properly describes or even understands. The style may change slightly, becoming more and more murmuring and deliquesced until it reaches the Unnamable's endlessly long sentences—comma after comma after comma—and his single closing 112-page paragraph; but the controlling presence changes not at all. In the end, what comes across most strongly is the effort of it all: the sheer hard labor of writing and the author's distaste for the whole miserable, pointless business. It is as though he had condemned himself to six years of forced labor during which he transformed himself by pure will power from a brilliant dilettante into a major artist.

In the earlier novels obsessionality was a mannerism and, sometimes, a source of wit. In the trilogy the obsession is single and altogether more serious. Beckett is creating his own death in prose, quarrying right down to that subterranean country of his heart, the country of what Coleridge called Life-in-Death, a landscape so sterile and impotent that nothing moves except the writer's hand across the page as he takes down dictation from his unstoppable voices. The trilogy is, quite literally, a *mémoire d'outre tombe* for our time. This becomes obvious when the three novels are read, as they were clearly written and have subsequently been published, as three parts of a single work. Together they constitute an undeviating withdrawal from both the exterior world and, it goes without saying, the traditional novel in which that world has always been reflected.

What remains is a terminal vision, a terminal style and, from the point of view of possible development, a work at least as aesthetically terminal as *Finnegans Wake*.

MOLLOY

Of all the distractions Beckett seemed concerned to overcome, the most formal was plot. On these terms *Molloy* is the most traditional of the trilogy, but even in *Molloy* plot swiftly collapses not into a stream of consciousness, with all it implies of free association, but into the vague yet continually precise subliminal mutter that was first tested in *Watt* and eventually became Beckett's narrative style. The book begins with Molloy shut away in his dead mother's room, steadily writing. Each week he is visited by a stranger who takes away what he has written and pays him money. So much for the mechanics of his subsistence. What he has written is, as it were, the preliminary to where he is now, a description of his long, fruitless odyssey in search of his mother.

He begins "crouched like Belacqua" in the shadow of a rock watching two men, A and C, approach each other across a plain. One carries a stout stick, the other —or is it the same?—is followed by a dog. Molloy is not sure whether they are travelers or mere strollers: "Did he not seem rather to have issued from the ramparts, after a good dinner, to take his dog and himself for a walk, like so many citizens, dreaming and farting, when the weather is fine?" The two men come together for a moment, peer together toward the distant sea, speak together briefly, and then separate, "A back towards the town, C on byways he seemed hardly to know." Molloy remembers them right at the end of his narrative; perhaps they were the reason he gave up the slothful comfort of his rock and set out, since they

showed him that motion was possible. Here at the beginning they serve as an image of two ways of going
to be brooded upon as he himself prepares to set out on
his quest for his mother.

Molloy's own journey is less easy than A's or C's. He
has a stiff leg which prevents him from walking properly, so he travels by bicycle, his crutches strapped to
the crossbar. He is harried by the police for the peculiarly
Beckettian crime of resting on his bicycle in a public
place—a public highway, in fact—and is almost lynched
by a mob when he runs over and kills a small dog. He
is rescued by the dog's owner, a fading charmer called
Lousse, which is an appropriate name considering her
wealthy but *louche* way of life. She adopts him and
pampers him like her dear deceased pet until he can
stand no more. He escapes her claustrophobic concern,
taking with him a few small items of silver, like the
hero of *Les Misérables*, but leaving his bicycle. He
moves now on crutches, becoming continually more
lame; the stiff leg becomes shorter, the good leg goes
stiff. He spends a comparatively happy time in a cave
by the seashore where he struggles with the Wattesque
problem of his sixteen sucking-stones and four pockets.
Moving with more and more difficulty, he reaches a
forest where he violently repulses and almost kills a
lonely woodcutter. After that he can no longer maintain his vertical stance; he crawls doggedly on through
the forest using his crutches as grapnels. At least one
cycle of the seasons has been completed. As spring
begins again he ends in a ditch at the edge of the forest,
a plain before him on which he can see—or thinks he
can see—"faintly outlined against the horizon, the
towers and steeples of a town, which of course I could
not assume was mine." He is vaguely wondering how he
will cross the bare plain—"rolling perhaps"—when he
hears a voice:

> Don't fret, Molloy, we're coming. Well, I suppose you
> have to try everything once, succour included, to get
> a complete picture of the resources of their planet.
> I lapsed down to the bottom of the ditch. . . . Molloy
> could stay, where he happened to be.

And that is that, except we know from the beginning
that help will come, although too late for him to find
his mother before she dies.

The second half of the novel is the same story again
from the opposite point of view. Where Molloy is like
his predecessor, Watt—vague, destitute, helpless, crip-
pled, and much given to pointless chop-logic—Moran,
the narrator of the second part, is clear-cut, a man of
will, action, and menace, and a chronic sufferer from
Habit, that symptom of the Time cancer. He is a
fanatic of religious and domestic routine who keeps a
brutal grip on his two dependents—a sullen pubescent
son and an equally resentful old woman servant. Like
Molloy, he is mad, but in a very different way: his
obsessionality is paranoid, expressing itself in petty
sadism and rigid control. He takes his pleasures in the
most tightly bourgeois ways: in churchgoing, food, a
well-ordered small holding, and a little furtive mastur-
bation. His only real feeling is for his hens, his bees,
and his garden. In other words, Moran is Pozzo to
Molloy's Lucky. Like Pozzo, he even considers tying
his cowed son to him with a rope.

Hugh Kenner has made the brilliant suggestion that
"Molloy and Moran are more or less the author's Irish
and French selves respectively."[5] Certainly, the style
bears him out. After Molloy's convolutions and obliqui-
ties, hesitations and hallucinations, Moran comes as a
great relief. His narrative moves swiftly and logically,
in short, crisp sentences. It is a model of everything
that the French, with their idealization of reason and

[5] *Op. cit.*, p. 57.

clarity, have ever imagined themselves to be. Although the two men finish in much the same decrepit condition, just as Pozzo ends blind and even more helpless than his slave, Moran's terse, matter-of-fact style never wavers. It is a tone appropriate to his calling; he is a slightly sinister private agent working for Youdi, a remote and powerful figure who reveals himself only through his messenger, Gaber. It is Gaber who arrives one comfortable afternoon with orders for Moran to leave immediately and hunt down Molloy. Gaber offers no explanations and Moran demands none; the hunter needs no reason for pursuing his quarry. So, just as Molloy had done, Moran in his turn sets out on a quest, accompanied by his surly child. And, like Molloy, the quest acts on him like a poison; his ordered life disintegrates around him, his defenses fall, he becomes contaminated by his quarry, "dispossessed of self." Like Beckett's other narrators, he is at times confused with his author, claiming credit for earlier creations:

> What a rabble in my head, what a gallery of moribunds. Murphy, Watt, Yerk, Mercier and all the others. . . . Stories, stories. I have not been able to tell them. I shall not be able to tell this one.

But it is Molloy, above all, who takes him over: like Molloy, he loses the use of his legs and has to roll and drag himself along; like Molloy, he violently assaults a stranger who accosts him in the woods; he ends, like Molloy, ruined. All that remains to him is his clear voice and raging tenacity:

> The more things resist me the more rabid I get. With time, and nothing but my teeth and nails, I would rage up from the bowels of the earth to its crust, knowing full well I had nothing to gain.

When his legs go he grimly continues his quest, perched helplessly on the back of a bicycle, while his son pedals.

Eventually, the child abandons him and Gaber reappears with orders from Youdi: "Moran, Jacques, home, instanter." Youdi has also sent a Keatsian message: "Life is a thing of beauty . . . and a joy for ever." "Do you think he meant human life?" asks the prostrate Moran. But there is no answer.

During the long crucifixion of his journey home, Moran solaces himself by pondering absurd questions of theology. When he finally arrives his neat property has gone to ruin, his beloved hens and bees are dead. He finishes as a recluse, on crutches, talking to the wild birds and listening to a voice in his head which speaks a language he does not know but is gradually learning. Molloy is similarly wrecked, although in more comfortable circumstances. Both are busy scribbling away at their reports. Despite everything, they have never met.

The parallels between Molloy and Moran seem to hint at some large, vague, allegorical intention—perhaps something to do with all those ludicrous but traditional theological puzzles Moran trots out toward the book's end. The names also seem ripe for interpretation: does Youdi echo Hebrew *Jahweh*, or German *Jude*, or English *you* with a French diminuitive ending? Is the messenger Gaber really Gabriel? It is doubtful. Beckett has always followed his first master and used names with which Joycean games can be played: Knott, Watt, Malone (man alone), Mahood (son of God), Macmann (son of man). Kenner points out that the characters in *Endgame* could be a hammer and three nails: Hamm, Clov (French *clou*), Nagg (German *nagel*), and Nell (*nail*). Godot in particular has provoked a positive fury of scholasticism: English *God* plus French *eau* (water)? Or *God* with a French diminuitive, as in Charlot, Chaplin's affectionate French name? Or *Godo*, which is spoken Irish for "God"? Beckett himself uncharacteristically got into the act when he reminded Hugh Kenner that there was a professional racing cyclist called Godeau. No doubt it is all good academic fun, but one should hang on to Beckett's own words at the end of *Watt*: "no symbols where none intended." To like puns, particularly learned and philosophical ones, is different from purveying grand metaphysical messages.

Beckett is not an allegorist; he simply looks allegorical in lieu of anything else—because, that is, he has never been interested in plots, nor had much talent for them. "Dante and the Lobster" and *Murphy* are the only works in which all the ends are tied together. Even in the plays he manages the impossible and avoids plots. Vivien Mercier described *Godot* as a work in which "nothing happens, twice." In the novels nothing happens, endlessly. His narrators tell stories—their own or other people's—contemptuously, in order to stave off their depression, or pass the time until death silences them, or simply to show they can do so, like Beckett himself grimly mastering the blank sheets of paper by sheer will power for six long years. "What a story," says Molloy, speaking for them all. "God send I don't make a balls of it." In the later novels the narrators are continually breaking off in utter boredom, disgusted by their own persistence and longwindedness. But what else can they do, since their fate is to write and write? Hence those larger, apparently allegorical meanings are, it would seem, merely haphazard; they are the more or less random effects of Beckett's overeducation. He cannot help being allusive, given a lifetime of intense but probably not very systematic reading, which in his sour maturity no longer seemed to amount to anything significant. The uncrowned king of *Malone Dies* is a parrot whose owner tries to make it repeat *"nihil in intellectu quod non prius in sensu."* After years of effort he can only squawk *"nihil in intellectu."*

"Nihil in intellectu" is a motto the allegorists would do well to remember. Beckett is a genuine existentialist

in that everything he writes returns, however regretfully, to the insight that there are no final answers to be had from theology or metaphysics. Perhaps this is at the root of his depression. The impotence his deprived, ruined characters sense so keenly and return to so consistently is spiritual as well as physical.

In short, the parallels between the two halves of *Molloy* are only casually meaningful. Molloy and Moran both set forth on their different odysseys, but the real quest happens ultimately inside the author's own skull. The exterior details are merely excuses for exploring two ways of reaching the same state of collapse. It is not so much a novel as two arias, two utterly disparate voices gradually coming together in one dissonant, dotty chime.

MALONE DIES

Malone Dies is a stage further into the darkness: there is one voice, less plot and an octogenarian narrator who keeps harping, with pride, on his impotence. He is in an even worse state than Molloy or Moran: he is bedridden, dying, wanting to die. Like Molloy, he does not know how he reached the room he is entombed in, although he has a blood-stained club at his bedside and vague memories of a forest and a blow on the head, so he might be the man either Molloy or Moran met and attacked in their wanderings, or he might be the traveler C whom Molloy saw before he set out. But it hardly matters, for Beckett takes these clues no further; they are merely gestures toward a kind of continuity he is no longer interested in.

In fact, the book's only continuity is, as its title implies, that of Malone's dying. He lies sourly in bed, occasionally rummaging through his paltry belongings, which he gathers to him with a hooked stick. Otherwise, his needs are basic and anonymously attended to:

"What matters is to eat and excrete. Dish and pot, dish and pot, these are the poles." Needless to say, he also writes; it is his one distraction, his only method of whiling away the tedium of waiting for the end. He begins telling himself the story of an adolescent called Saposcat (Homo sapiens plus scatological, suggests Hugh Kenner), who hangs around the brute family of a farmer called Lambert. When that tale bores him, which is soon enough, he shifts to Macmann, a Watt-like hobo first seen disintegrating in the busy despair of a modern city, then removed to yet another of those Beckett lunatic asylums, the House of St. John of God. There, he is nursed and solaced by Moll, an old crone who has the crucifixion engraved on her one remaining tooth. In her dank embrace Macmann achieves "a kind of sombre gratification," despite his impotence. But Moll dies, leaving her lover in the sadistic care of Lemuel. The book ends when the do-good Lady Pedal takes Lemuel and his charges on an excursion to an island. There, Lemuel runs beserk with a hatchet, murdering two men and leaving Lady Pedal injured. He then puts out to sea with his mad but docile patients. As the boat drifts away into the night, Macmann and his creator Malone die in unison:

> Gurgles of outflow.
> This tangle of grey bodies is they. Silent, dim, perhaps clinging to one another, their heads buried in their cloaks, they lie together in a heap, in the night. They are far out in the bay. Lemuel has shipped his oars, the oars trail in the water. The night is strewn with absurd
> absurd lights, the stars, the beacons, the buoys, the lights of earth and in the hills the faint fires of the blazing gorse. Macmann, my last, my possessions, I remember, he is there too, perhaps he sleeps. Lemuel
> Lemuel is in charge, he raises his hatchet on which the blood will never dry, but not to hit anyone, he will

not hit anyone, he will not hit anyone any more, he
will not touch anyone any more, either with it or
with it or with it or with or
    or with it or with his hammer or with his stick or
with his fist or in thought in dream I mean never he
will never
    or with his pencil or with his stick or
    or light light I mean
    never there he will never
    never anything
    there
    any more

The mannerism of the earlier books has gone. Beckett
has finally perfected a bare and supple style wholly
his own, the concentration that once went into elaborat-
ing his dandified rhetoric turned now to the demands
of austerity and precision. There is no gap between the
style and the subject: the prose is that of a man at his
last gasp, halting, tentative, his mind slipping away,
rousing itself to further effort, failing again and again
ever more swiftly. Malone drifts out into death as the
boat drifts aimlessly into darkness. And as he does so,
his mind closes repeatedly and with relief on a single
blessing: "he will not hit anyone any more, he will not
touch anyone any more." The punishment of life is
over, a punishment to which Beckett, too, has contributed his share, since Malone's pencil is confused
with Lemuel's hatchet, stick, and fist.

It is a passage "of great formal brilliance" and also
of beauty. And this is typical of all Beckett's novels
from *Watt* onward; sooner or later the obsessions and
complaining cease and the author devotes his attention,
however briefly, to the outside world. In *Watt* there is
an extraordinary description of the cycle of the year;
Molloy allows himself to discourse hauntingly on night
sounds and even Moran glimpses a pastoral idyll of a
shepherd and his dog; *Malone Dies* has a *Waste Land*

vision of a modern city, a number of exquisite passages describing Lambert and his animals, and this moment of release for the abused young Sapo:

> But he loved the flight of the hawk and could distinguish it from all others. He would stand rapt, gazing at the long pernings, the quivering poise, the wings lifted for the plummet drop, the wild reascent, fascinated by such extremes of need, of pride, of patience and solitude.

There is nothing in Beckett's poetry so sharply felt or so accurately and dispassionately seen as this; it is one of the most curious aspects of the novels that although his theme is a depression deepening to the point of death and annihilation, it provides him nevertheless with occasions for indulging his senses, his aesthetic powers of invocation, and his amazingly precise observation of that natural world which lies outside the minutiae of gloom, bowels, and obsession to which the novels are otherwise devoted. To produce this passage about the hawk required not only great skill, but also great love. It makes Beckett's deliberate rejection of the natural world seem doubly painful.

In *Malone Dies* these moments of illumination and pleasure are rare. Most of the time Beckett's theme works against traditional aesthetic perfection. The purer his negation and less quenchable his despair, the impurer the construction. The plot keeps vanishing, everything is left in the air and the only thread tied is that of Malone's life. Even so, the book is strangely eloquent. This is partly a matter of the unwavering clarity of the writing. Although *Malone Dies* is a monologue, it is not a Joycean stream of consciousness. In fact, it could not be, since a stream of consciousness implies all the human clutter that Beckett is trying at last to eliminate. Molloy, Malone, and those who come after, as well as the people they talk about, belong to Murphy's world:

that of the utterly deprived, of those who seem orphaned at birth, who turn their backs in abhorrence on emotion. All that stands between them and chaos is their considerable learning and their language. And their language reflects their learning; it is disciplined, precise, allusive, at times tending to pedantry. The one quality that defines them all, as they speak, is their meticulousness. Despite themselves, they cannot help being coherent. This persists even in the most terminal of all the novels, *How It Is*, which manages to remain comprehensible while dispensing with all the traditional props of clarity, including punctuation.

Malone Dies is not only eloquent, it also achieves in its closing pages a weird and haunting peace. It is partly the peace of aesthetic nihilism: the author has destroyed the traditional novel at last and cleared a way through to his later experiments with the metanovel. But it is partly the peace of total personal negation. Nothing remains. Death has resolved the last and most abiding of all the obsessions that plague Beckett's gallery of smelly, ugly, crotchety ancients; I mean their obsession with guilt:

> And without knowing exactly what his sin was he felt full well that living was not a sufficient atonement for it or that this atonement was in itself a sin, calling for more atonement, and so on, as if there could be anything but life, for the living. And no doubt he would have wondered if it was really necessary to be guilty in order to be punished but for the memory, more and more galling, of his having consented to live in his mother, than to leave her. And this again he could not see as his true sin, but as yet another atonement which had miscarried and, far from cleansing him of his sin, plunged him in it deeper than before. And truth to tell the ideas of guilt and punishment were confused together in his mind, as those

of cause and effect so often are in the minds of those who continue to think.

Later Malone says this again more brusquely: "No matter, any old remains of flesh and spirit will do, there is no sense in stalking people. So long as it is what is called a living being you can't go wrong, you have the guilty one." Beckett's characters may occasionally be given to pondering insoluble theological problems and paradoxes, but Beckett has solved to his own satisfaction the most basic Christian problem of all: as he announced in the essay on Proust, the real original sin is life itself. Macmann reflects with relief that "his semen had never done any harm to anyone," and Malone takes pride in his impotence. This seems, in the circumstances, the nearest either will ever attain to virtue. Perhaps this is why Beckett in his turn protects himself from the authorial charge of having given his characters life by the strategy of formlessness, the aesthetic equivalent of impotence. So everything in *Malone Dies* is reduced to a voice, rambling, unemphatic, sometimes plangent, more often irritated by "all this ballsaching poppycock about life and death," but always enervated beyond enervation. It is the voice of a man who has given up and is sustained only by the imminence of death, as he writes on and on in his un-visited room. "The end of a life," says Malone, "is always vivifying." The peace the novel finally attains is that of extinction patiently longed for. *Malone Dies* ends when Malone is dead.

THE UNNAMABLE

En Attendant Godot was written "d'une traite" between October 1948 and the end of January 1949—that is, between *Malone Meurt* and *L'Innommable*. Apparently, life went on for Beckett, if not for his characters. But in *Malone* the already fragile distinction between the narrator and Beckett himself had largely disintegrated. Both Molloy and Moran refer to their predecessors in the canon as though they themselves were the author; in *Malone* this *trompe l'œil* technique is taken much further. As was mentioned earlier, Beckett continually uses the natural breaks in writing—when he got up to eat or sleep, or took a weekend off—as part of his narrative: "What a misfortune," says Malone. "The pencil must have slipped from my fingers, for I have only just succeeded in recovering it after forty-eight hours." This is like Brecht's notorious "alienation effect," a way of keeping the created characters at a distance and the audience dispassionate, analytical, uninvolved. Like the people in Beckett's plays, Malone is constantly breaking in on his own story with such comments as "What tedium" or "This is awful." To the dread boredom of life and habit, which Beckett made so much of in his Proust essay, is added the supreme boredom of writing itself. But at another level this style of literary double-shuffle is also a protest against the false conventions of fiction, against "the whole sorry business, I mean the business of Malone (since that is what I am called now)." The note is weary, a little contemptuous, which is not surprising considering the degree of depression Beckett is probing in the trilogy. Ultimately, it is this depression that breaks down the barriers between creator and created. Malone contemplating the nearness of death literally becomes Beckett pondering all the characters he has killed off in his novels:

> Let us leave these morbid matters and get on with that of my demise, in two or three days if I remember rightly. Then it will be all over with the Murphys, Merciers, Molloys, Morans and Malones, unless it

goes on beyond the grave. But sufficient unto the day,
let us first defunge, then we'll see. How many have I
killed, hitting them on the head or setting fire to
them? Off-hand I can only think of four, all un-
knowns, I never knew anyone. . . . There was the
old butler too, in London I think, there's London
again, I cut his throat with his razor, that makes
five.[6]

The effect is cinematic, the face of Malone continually
dissolving into that of Beckett, then out again, like a
light pulsing slowly and irregularly.

Even more than the earlier heroes, Malone exists
not in his own right but simply as a mask Beckett can
pick up and put down again as it suits him. Yet Beckett
himself remains remote and impersonal. However much
he talks in his own person, he is careful to say nothing
compromising. The reader learns nothing at all of his
life and little enough of his habit of mind beyond his
bored distaste for his own dogged hard work. Beckett
exists only as a voice beyond or behind the narrator's
voice, far off but pervasive, like the voices Mr. Endon
and Watt listened to so attentively in their madness.
The only difference is one of tone: despite every temptation, the voice remains scrupulous and cool, as though
meticulousness were its one frail link with sanity.

In *The Unnamable* even this distinction between
narrator and author begins to fail. *Malone Dies* retains
a few paltry shreds of plot, incident, and character
because it is an attempt at an ending; if the narrator
dies publicly, for all to read, perhaps the voices will
cease. As it turned out, Beckett's pessimism was too
profound to allow him to believe that death would be
an end or even a relief. The voices continue beyond

---

[6] The butler, incidentally, never even managed a walk-on
part in *Murphy*; his throat was cut off stage.

the grave, into the limbo, the "pit," where the Unnamable is fixed. And finally, they too begin to disintegrate.

Originally, *The Unnamable* was to be called *Mahood*, which is one of the names the speaker goes under; another alias, more appropriate to the grave, is Worm. Presumably, Beckett decided against this because a proper name implies a proper hero—however tenuously, given the ground prepared in the two previous novels— whereas *The Unnamable* accurately describes the unfocused, indeterminate nature of the work. It is a single monologue—after the first dozen pages a single paragraph—from the underworld, spoken by a kind of preliminary creature, a protobeing "who came before the cross, before the sinning, came into the world, came here." Although he is aware of his feet and of his hands on his knees, he is without features or protuberances— no nose, no sex. He is smooth and hairless, "a big talking ball," wearing puttees and a few shreds of rag, unable to stir. He writes, of course, but how is a question he does not pursue. Otherwise, he is immobile, staring fixedly ahead with weeping, bloodshot eyes: "They must be as red as live coals." The limbo he inhabits is dark, with fitful gleams of light and no landmarks apart from the already dead Malone, revolving regularly around him like a moon. Like all Beckett's figures, the speaker is a man more or less without a past; he has been where he is since he, or time, began, although he has a certain amount of information, mostly forgotten or disregarded, about God, his mother, and his place of birth, "Bally I forget what." Essentially he has attained that posthumous existence for which all Beckett's heroes pined: "a little hell after my own heart, not too cruel, with a few nice damned to foist my groans on. . . . But even this promised bliss—after all, the irredeemably guilty, those guilty of the original sin of life, can be satisfied only in hell, heaven being reserved for the unborn—

brings no relief to his real torment: the inescapable need to go on talking. At one point he compares himself to Prometheus chained to his rock in the Caucasus. But for him the vulture gnawing eternally at his innards is language. He is condemned to words as ineluctably as any sinner in Dante's Inferno is condemned to his own special torment. He repeats this, in one way or another, again and again; it is both his obsession and his novelist's task:

> All these Murphys, Molloys and Malones do not fool me. They have made me waste my time, suffer for nothing, speak of them when, in order to stop speaking, I should have spoken of me and me alone.

". . . *in order to stop speaking*": in other words, he writes in order to absolve himself of the need to write, just as the sinner suffers in hell in order to redeem his sins on earth. His unattainable quietus is silence.

As usual, Beckett tries telling stories, although sporadically now and without conviction. There is a long passage about his—or Mahood's—life in an urn outside a restaurant, the menu pinned below his head, plagued by bluebottles from the nearby slaughterhouse. It is a situation like that of *Play*, although without the edge or intensity. In *Play*, too, the three characters—man, wife, and mistress—are in some kind of hell: encased in urns, heads fixed, they rattle on compulsively, bitterly, whenever an interrogating beam of light strikes them. But they have, at least, human faces and are talking, at least, about a human enough situation, adultery. In *The Unnamable*, the only real subject is the words themselves and the intolerable need to use them, but as the book progresses even the words lose their tenuous connection with reality. The sentences become more fragmentary and run on increasingly swiftly until there is only a smeared impression of a mind dilating and expanding, deliquescing in horror, fear, and disgust around its own misery: "tottering under my own skin and bones, real ones, rotting with solitude and neglect, till I doubted my own existence, and even still, today, I have no faith in it, none." This is like Hamlet's soliloquies without the Prince, King, Queen, attendant lords, or plot, the soliloquies spoken by the Ghost who has long ago ceased to care about his revenge, since he knows that nothing will redeem him from his particular hell.

As the words batter on about nothing except themselves and their speaker's despair, and the sentences gather momentum until they run for pages on end, the voice thickens into genuine madness. From beneath that mixture of weariness, distaste, and blind determination to get it all down, which dominated the tone of the earlier parts of the trilogy, there emerges in the end a note of pure panic. Molloy once confessed:

> The truth is . . . I felt more or less the same as usual, that is to say, if I may give myself away, so terror-stricken that I was virtually bereft of feeling, not to say of consciousness, and drowned in a deep and merciful torpor shot with brief abominable gleams, I give you my word.

This sounds like the state of mind of a chronic schizophrenic: at once panic-stricken and torpid, the torpor defending him from the panic. Yet Molloy, like Malone, remains so sturdily wry, coherent, and resigned to his own gross ineptitude that, without his word for it, his inner life might have been difficult to guess. Not so the Unnamable; he may speak of despair but it is terror that comes through most strongly because reality recedes as he speaks, as if the words were disintegrating in his mouth. Grammar of a kind remains, but the language itself loses whatever minimal substantiality it still retained after Beckett abjured people and plots. Perhaps this is how the crazy inner voices sounded

when they besieged the sanity of Watt and Mr. Endon—
autonomous, insidious, unstoppable. But in *The Unnamable* Beckett has deliberately destroyed the distinction between his narrator and himself.

The book finishes with the speaker still not reassured,
still not at peace, condemned still to talk:

> perhaps it's a dream, all a dream, that would surprise
> me, I'll wake, in the silence, and never sleep again,
> it will be I, or dream, dream again, dream of a silence,
> a dream silence, full of murmurs, I don't know, that's
> all words, never wake, all words, there's nothing
> else, you must go on, that's all I know, they're going
> to stop, I know that well, I can feel it, they're going
> to abandon me, it will be the silence, for a moment,
> a good few moments, or it will be mine, the lasting
> one, that didn't last, that still lasts, it will be I, you
> must go on, I can't go on, you must go on, I'll go
> on, you must say words, as long as there are any, until
> they find me, until they say me, strange pain, strange
> sin, you must go on, perhaps it's done already, per-
> haps they have said me already, perhaps they have
> carried me to the threshold of my story, before the
> door that opens on my story, that would surprise me,
> if it opens, it will be I, it will be the silence, where
> I am, I don't know, I'll never know, in the silence
> you don't know, you must go on, I can't go on, I'll go
> on.

It has been said that the note at the end is somehow
hopeful, that he is speaking for the indomitability of
the human spirit. Perhaps. But coming at the end of a
vast, scattered sentence which closes a paragraph of
over 112 pages, it seems that the words, "you must go
on, I can't go on, I'll go on," sound less like an affirmation than a threat. However inexhaustible a mother
lode for quarrying academics the book may be, for the
ordinary, even devoted reader, *The Unnamable* gets
perilously close to being the Unreadable.

"You've been sufficiently assassinated," says the narrator, "sufficiently suicided, to be able to stand on your own feet, like a big boy." In a way, this was the purpose of the whole trilogy. Technically, it is a stage-by-stage assassination of the novel in all the forms in which it is traditionally received. The last part of the work is a novel only by virtue of being a long piece of more or less imaginative prose. In that sense, Beckett was using the novel form only in order to go beyond it, as he had already gone beyond poetry, using it as a clearinghouse in which he could unclutter himself of his obsessions and so be free to move on into another form, the drama. But the themes of assassination and suicide are also rooted in the mid-life crisis; by coming to terms with one's depression and destructiveness, the theory goes, one may eventually come to accept one's mortality. But that has never quite seemed to be Beckett's problem. As I said before, depression and a kind of spiritual decrepitude seem always to have been as natural to his condition as being Irish or having blue eyes: "that childhood said to have been mine the difficulty of believing in it," confesses the narrator of *How It Is*; "the feeling rather of having been born octogenarian at the age when one dies in the mud in the dark." This is probably why all the novels, however deviously or ironically, always return to one form or another of madness, as though it were a subject he cannot escape. In the trilogy there is no question of accepting his depression and going beyond it; instead, it represents an attempt to perfect an art form in which he could, at least symbolically, die. Not only is death and Life-in-Death his subject, it is also his form: all human detail is stripped away, leaving only the aesthetic equivalent of "a big talking ball," an art form bereft of everything except the basic *donné* of literature, language.

"Strange pain, strange sin": there is no doubting the agony of a man condemned, for reasons he does not understand, to an eternity in the hell of words. The problem is that the expression of this torment is, artistically speaking, self-defeating. The greater the agony, the greater the prolixity. Despite the meticulousness of the writing and the taut control of tone, *The Unnamable* runs on so long, so remorselessly, and with so little real variation that it seems in the end self-indulgent and, like most self-indulgence, wasteful. In *Endgame* Hamm has one brief speech which in ten lines encapsulates, vividly and finally, the whole horrified vision *The Unnamable* struggles for in more than a hundred pages:

> I once knew a madman who thought the end of the world had come. He was a painter—and engraver. I had a great fondness for him. I used to go and see him, in the asylum. I'd take him by the hand and drag him to the window. Look! There! All that rising corn! And there! Look! The sails of the herring fleet! All that loveliness! (*Pause.*) He'd snatch away his hand and go back into his corner. Appalled. All he had seen was ashes. (*Pause.*) He alone had been spared. (*Pause.*) Forgotten. (*Pause.*) It appears the case is . . . was not so . . . so unusual.

It may be that this speech was prepared for and made possible by the gloomy labor of the novel, but compared to it *The Unnamable* seems flaccid and redundant. It seems a classic case of a work that is necessary but not sufficient; that is to say, necessary to Beckett personally in his exploration of his own limitless negation, but artistically insufficient because of its length, repetitiveness, and private claustrophobia. In the end, it seems less a triumph or art or will than an ungainly, sprawling monument to Beckett's abiding threefold obsession—with language, impotence, and death.

HOW IT IS

Beckett worked on the trilogy from 1947 to 1950. From 1950 to 1952 came *Textes pour rien*, a series of thirteen free variations on themes from *The Unnamable*, written in the same breathless, bodiless style. Then after three years during which he wrote nothing and a period during which he turned exclusively to drama— *Endgame*, *All That Fall*, *Krapp's Last Tape*, *Embers*— he returned to the novel in 1960, when he wrote *How It Is*.

On the face of it, it looks as though Beckett had decided, after more than eight years away from the form, that the novel had not, after all, been "sufficiently assassinated, sufficiently suicided"; so he wrote *How It Is* in order to finish the job. In *The Unnamable* he had dispensed with paragraphs and, to an extraordinary extent, with full stops. In *How It Is* he keeps the paragraphs but dispenses with all punctuation. Each chunk of prose becomes a spasm of blind effort overtaken by exhaustion, while within the paragraphs the prose moves in short phrases gasped out brokenly by the narrator, each the span of a single breath. I suppose it is a mark of his general dereliction that he continually pants out the same phrases: "long past long gone," "vast stretch of time," "I say it as I hear it," "quaqua," "something wrong there," "the panting stops," and so on. These "bits and scraps" (another favorite) are presumably the only certainties he has left; he brings them out as if to reassure himself.

At first glance, *How It Is* might seem just another unlovable form of experiment, carried out at that fine front edge of the most advanced guard where the distinction between poetry and prose is blurred into indifference. But there are three important distinctions between Beckett's practice here and the general mess of more conventional, dog-eared experimentation. First,

Beckett never abandons his meticulousness. As a result, despite its formidable appearance the work is always coherent, once the reader has laboriously tuned in to its difficult wave length. Even at its most disintegrated, when the shattered syntax is scarcely that of the gasp, there is a kind of clenched lucidity about Beckett's writing that somehow justifies one's efforts. Unlike, say, Pound's late Cantos, there is nothing slapdash or willful in *How It Is*, and no trace of impossible private references. With patience and concentration, the reader need never be at a loss. The difficulties are all public and resolvable.

Second, and related to this, the style can at times rise to great brilliance:

> reread our notes / pass the time / more about me than him / hardly a word out of him now / not a / mum this past year and more / I lose the nine-tenths / it starts so sudden / comes so faint / goes so fast / ends so soon / I'm on it / in a flash it's over[7]

Beckett is using prose here to catch something transient in the actual process of its passing. His prose is like a piece of kinetic art, constantly shifting, changing, stirring, yet worked out with infinite care and precision.

Third, the style is appropriate to the situation portrayed in the book. It is not so much unpunctuated as beyond punctuation, just as the speaker is beyond any form of reasonable life we know or can imagine. In a way, it follows from Beckett's previous novel. One of the names the Unnamable briefly allowed himself was Worm; *How It Is* is a worm's eye view of the afterlife. The speaker, who compares himself to Belacqua, is face down in a world of mud and darkness through which he drags himself painfully forward for ever, ten or fifteen yards at a time, pulling after him a coalsack full of supplies—tins of sardines and a tin-opener—

[7] For this first example pause marks have been put in.

which is tied closed by a rope attached in turn to his neck. As he goes he mutters to himself, "quaqua," "quaqua," "I say it as I hear it." It is Beckett's perennial image of the novelist as a living corpse, totally isolated, listening to voices: "I say it as I hear it." Previously there had been some, though increasingly vague, attempts to manipulate these voices and make them tell stories. Now they have become wholly internal; that is to say, they have become what they always were: simply voices, no more, no less. At the end of the book Beckett admits in despair that they have always been his own. Without acknowledging it, he has been listening only to himself; there has never been anyone else:

> but all this business of voices yes quaqua yes of other worlds yes of someone in another world yes whose kind of dream I am yes said to be yes that he dreams all the time yes tells all the time yes his only dream yes his only story yes . . . all balls

This realization that the voices have no source outside himself leads to a further understanding: that he is "alone in the mud yes the dark yes." To which his final, appalled and, God knows, uncharacteristic response is a scream of terror: "I SHALL DIE." But as usual, death is too easy a release and once again is indefinitely postponed. The end of the book, like that of *Finnegans Wake*, circles back to the beginning; the last words of the original French version are *comment c'est*, which, as a number of commentators have pointed out, is a pun on *commencer*.

Needless to say, there is no plot to speak of. The book is in three parts: before Pim, with Pim, after Pim. Before Pim there is only the speaker dragging his sack remorselessly through the mud and darkness, occasionally eating, occasionally resting, occasionally sucking the mud for sustenance and pleasure, as old

Malone sucked at his bedclothes, and all the while
gasping out the disjointed, breathless phrases that de-
fine his condition: "hanging on by the finger-nails to
one's species." Every so often a fully formed memory
of "life in the light" bursts to the surface like a perfect,
brilliant bubble: a pastoral idyll of himself, aged sixteen, walking in the country with a girl and a dog; another of himself as a small child saying his prayers
at his mother's knee, "the huge head hatted with birds
and flowers is bowed down over my curls the eyes burn
with severe love."[8] Later there are grimmer memories
of a marriage that failed as the sex waned, the wife
finally jumping out of a window and dying of her
injuries, and also memories of a beloved dog run over
by a dray, and of jobs the speaker took, mostly in the
building trade. Each memory cuts off abruptly, like a
door slamming shut—"that's all it goes out like a lamp
blown out"—leaving the narrator where he was, face
down and desolate in the slime.

In Part Two he comes up with Pim, another sufferer
in the mud. They grapple, arms and legs entwined like
a pair of amorous primeval reptiles, and crawl together
for a while. Infinitely slowly, over "vast stretches of
time" and pages, they evolve a satisfying Pavlovian
relationship of sadist and victim. It is a long condi-
tioning by cruelty in which the speaker somehow
manages to communicate with Pim by clawing his
armpit, sticking the blade of the tin-opener into his
rectum, and thumping his head into the mud:

> table of basic stimuli one sing nails in armpit two
> speak blade in arse three stop thump on skull four
> louder pestle on kidney

[8] There is a photograph of a scene like this in John Calder,
Beckett at 60 (London, 1967), p. 24. It is the earliest known
photograph of Beckett.

five softer index in anus six bravo clap athwart arse
seven lousy same as three eight encore same as one
or two

He also tries writing on Pim's palm, although without
results. This relationship with Pim reminds him, appropriately enough, of his suicide wife. Afterlife in the
posthumous slime is essentially no different from life
up there in the light; it is, he says, "sadism pure and
simple."[9]

In Part Three, when Pim moves away at last, the
speaker slowly realizes that, despite appearances, he is
not alone. He in his turn is awaiting Bom, who will
treat him as he has treated Pim. All of them are part
of an infinite number of damned, moving blindly
through the mud in a great chain of torment:

> and these same couples that eternally form and form
> again all along this immense circuit that the mil-
> lionth time that's conceivable is as the inconceivable
> first and always two strangers uniting in the interests
> of torment

He can only cope with this unbearable knowledge, like
Watt, by page after page of calculation, juggling with
the numbers of tormentors and tormented, their sacks
of food, positions, and possible movements. In the end
even this last crazy defense collapses and he is left
with the understanding that everything—voices, victims,
tormentors—exists only in his own head; it is all a
fantasy, "all balls." Death is ready to pounce. But it
does not; instead, the cycle begins again: *da capo ad
inf.*

[9] Similarly, toward the end of *The Unnamable*, as his
depression and panic increase, the narrator begins to cast
around for "signs of life." All he can come up with is
sadistic fantasies: "the little cry that frogs give when the
scythe slices them in half, or when they are spiked, in their
pools, with a spear, one could multiply the examples."

It was suggested that *How It Is* represents Beckett's ultimate attempt to assassinate the novel. Perhaps this does him an injustice. The traditional novel was, after all, "sufficiently assassinated" by the end of the trilogy. *How It Is* is the dismemberment of a corpse. All that remains of the ordinary novel are the most basic elements: imaginative prose about some kind of talking, if not quite living, creature, and a skeleton plot. On this conventional level, the book seems not only impossibly difficult—nothing happens, not twice but endlessly and with microscopic complexity—but also grotesquely pessimistic: the whole of life is reduced to "a migration of slime worms" relieved only by torment and brief memories of how it was "up there in the light." The gloom is so unwinking that, if Beckett were only fractionally less scrupulous a writer, it would seem mere affectation.

Yet given Beckett's habitual meticulousness of both style and feeling, given also that some kind of limbo or life-in-death has been the destination of all his efforts, given his real terminal depression, then the book gathers to itself a certain grandeur. Above all, it is an extraordinary tour de force. Using little more than a handful of stock phrases and a grammatical construction beyond syntax, Beckett manages to create an absolutely precise, absolutely lucid medium that responds instantly to each shift of attention and mood. It is the aesthetic equivalent of what scientists call "pure research."

Perhaps this is the clue to all Beckett's later prose works. They are the laboratories in which he carries out his experiments undisturbed by any audience. In comparison, his plays have always seemed relatively impure by his standards, because they involve a not wholly predictable element: human actors. In his prose, on the other hand, he is in complete control, answerable to no one, not even to that presumably small readership whom he has persistently treated with supreme take-it-or-leave-it indifference. His pure research is in two linked areas. First, there are his technical experiments in evolving a language without reverberations. This language is the opposite of that used by Joyce, who, in *Finnegans Wake*, produced a punster's paradise where every word cuts several ways at once, usually into several languages. Beckett, conversely, writes in a foreign language, translates it back into his own, and loses nothing in the transaction. He is left with a transparent medium drained of all local and associative color. He then manipulates this until it can contain the maximum tension and compression with the minimum weight and fuss. His language is the prose writer's equivalent of the advanced metallurgy of space flight: a medium that is neutral, almost weightless, yet able to withstand enormous stress.

The language without reverberations is appropriate to the other area in which he conducts his curious research: the emotions. I have suggested that the trilogy began with mid-life depression and a massive effort of the creative will, and ended with the creation of a form in which Beckett could, literally, inhabit his own death. It is a modern version of that alchemical distillation of emptiness and despair which John Donne described in "A nocturnall upon S. *Lucies* day":

> For I am every dead thing,
>   In whom love wrought new Alchimie.
>   For his art did expresse
> A quintessence even from nothingnesse,
> From dull privations, and leane emptinesse:
> He ruin'd me, and I am re-begot
> Of absence, darknesse, death; things which are not.

But there is a crucial difference between Donne's and Beckett's seemingly similar despair. Donne roots his in a specific social situation: the monstrous alchemist was love, the headlong marriage which had ruined his glittering career and thrust upon him the "dull privations, and leane emptinesse" of the long, penurious years before he took Holy Orders. Beckett's desolation, in contrast, is cut loose from reality and from that ubiquitous sense of worldly passion, ambition, and frustration which stirs just below the surface of everything Donne wrote. In the end, Beckett really does make one believe in the voices that haunt him so obsessively, for even his anguish is bodiless.

Although Beckett's desolation is self-generated, it is not self-regarding. No matter how persistently his narrators speak in the first person, no matter how contemptuous they may be of the names and disguises they put on for the sake of their stories, the impersonality of his writing is unremitting and iron-bound. It seems plausible, for example, that the opening pages of *Molloy* were added after the trilogy was finished and Beckett's own mother, like Molloy's, had died. But not only is it impossible to tell, it is also beside the point. There are no intimate references, because, as the novels repeat again and again, none are needed; the author is merely a servant of his voices, or rather their victim, condemned to an eternity of dictation. The worlds Beckett describes in his novels, at least from *Watt* on, are all internal landscapes. This is why the final revelation of *How It Is* carries such weight and horrified conviction: nothing, nothing at all, exists outside the narrator's own skull. It is a revelation to which all the earlier novels inescapably lead: Murphy's solipsism was whimsical, the diversion of an overeducated man bored and irritated by his threadbare, gossipy life; Watt's rambling obsessionality was a stage beyond this, a symptom of the gentle dottiness to which he eventually succumbed; in the trilogy the despair gradually gathered momentum until it became a full-blown psychosis, terror-stricken and helpless. *How It Is* has gone beyond that, not into death but catatonia: the narrator is blind and mute; he himself finally suggests that he may also be deaf when he realizes that all the voices he thought he heard, like the strange sadomasochistic tenderness between Pim and himself and the shards of memory of a feeling life "up there in the light," have no reality outside his own head. This leaves only him and the mud and darkness to which we all return in the end. It is a work of unique negation. Beckett's achievement is in expressing it with a corresponding purity, concentration, and originality, and without a trace of self-pity.

The Plays: Carry on Talking

111

However great the skill and austerity of Beckett's novels, their final effect is, both literally and deliberately, deadening. They are honed to such a fine point of bodiless desolation, so technically difficult, and so narrow in range, that it is doubtful they would be read by anyone except a few devotees and specialists were it not for the plays.

As if he had only a limited amount of energy to bestow on the outside world, Beckett did not turn to the stage until his novels had become abstract and unpeopled. No doubt it took all his attention to control the great weight of un-namable, intolerable depression pressing on his work like a reservoir against a dam; he could meter it out only by the unremitting strictness of his style and tone. Once Beckett began to write plays, the texture of his novels became more purely linguistic and their human content thinned out into that solipsism Murphy had found so congenial years before. In time the plays, too, have thinned away to mime and the interplay between minimal mime and minimal speech that he perfected in *Come and Go.* Even in his more expansive performances the actual presence of actors is not always necessary: *Krapp's Last Tape* and *Play* are as effective on radio as they are on the stage; *Eh Joe,* his television play, uses only a single camera, gradually moving in to tighter close-up on a single actor listening to someone else's voice, as though to the radio. In comparison, the two great early plays, *Godot* and *Endgame,* seem positively Chaucerian in their expansiveness and movement. Although the action is sparse, characters at least come and go, a tree puts out a few leaves, there are ladders to be climbed, windows to be peered from. "Here," as they say, "is God's plenty"—at least when compared with *Breath.* Naturally enough, Beckett used the freedom the huge success of his masterpieces gave him to become even more a minority writer than he had been before. It was only a matter of time before the acute shyness, said to be characteristic of the man himself, became in his art a total and contemptuous aloofness to his audience. The brevity and desolation of his later plays is as unforgiving as that of his novels.

WAITING FOR GODOT

Even *Godot* begins bleakly enough: "A country road. A tree. Evening." That is to say, the stage is bare except for a tree and the light is subdued. The opening words fit the setting and are, as it turns out, the theme of the play:

ESTRAGON: Nothing to be done.
VLADIMIR: I'm beginning to come round to that opinion.

Estragon is, in fact, referring to his boots. A little later
Vladimir repeats the phrase twice, first referring to his
hat, then to the uselessness of mirth. But essentially
they are both talking about their lives. The subject of
the play is how to pass the time, given the fact that the
situation is hopeless. In other words, it is a dramatization of the themes first aired in the essay on Proust and
then repeated continually throughout the novels: habit,
boredom, and "the suffering of being." "Habit," wrote
the snooty young academic, freshly graduated with
honors and polysyllabically determined to show it, "is
a compromise effected between the individual and his
environment, or between the individual and his own
organic eccentricities, the guarantee of dull inviolability,
the lightning conductor of his existence." At the end of
Godot Vladimir says the same thing more baldly and with
the whole weight of the play behind him: "Habit is a
great deadener." By then he and Estragon have had two
hours on stage to prove it. Although there are moments
in the play when "the suffering of being" has pierced
them both, neither comments on them: when Vladimir
tries to laugh, he stops immediately, "his face convulsed";
when the little boy comes to tell them Godot will not
appear that evening, Estragon attacks him, then relapses, covering his face with his hands; when he drops
his hands, "his face is convulsed"; "I'm unhappy" is all
he manages. The rest is mostly ritual, filling the emptiness and silence. "It'll pass the time," explains Vladimir,
offering to tell the story of the Crucifixion. In fact, passing the time is their mutual obsession. When Pozzo and
Lucky go off after their first appearance there is a long
silence. Then:

v: That passed the time.
e: It would have passed in any case.
v: Yes, but not so rapidly.

Yet immediately Estragon, too, joins in the game: "That's the idea, let's make a little conversation." He keeps at it fervently in the beginning of the second act: "That's the idea, let's contradict each other," "That's the idea, let's ask each other questions," "That wasn't such a bad little canter"; to which Vladimir replies, "Yes, but now we'll have to find something else." The idea of *Godot* as a play in which "nothing happens, twice" is understood by no one so sharply as by the tramps. Nothingness is what they are fighting against and why they talk.

The rituals by which they combat silence and emptiness are elaborate, original, and emerge directly out of Beckett's practice as a novelist. In order to handle the obsessionality that was both the defining characteristic and the sickness of his earlier heroes he needed a high degree of precision, an iron logic of madness. In the plays this precision goes into the echoing patterns of question, answer, and repetition which is his alternative to all the flaccid chat and triviality of the conventional "well-made play" before he arrived on the scene. Since his subject is habit and boredom, he can dispense with plot; since his characters are, as usual, without history, he can dispense with background. All that is left is a skeleton of language, logic, and wit. And by some perverse quirk of creativity what remains is more convincing and even more substantial than the conventions he is replacing and also than his own practice in the novels. The obsessionality that in *Watt* degenerated continually into demented pedantry is transformed in *Godot* into an elegant aural discipline for maintaining a dialogue when there is nothing to say.

The talk is kept going by a simple device: instant forgetfulness. Estragon, who quotes poetry, claims to be a poet, and has his rags to prove it, behaves more or less as though suffering brain damage. Like Watt, he is unable, or unwilling, to recognize the evidence of his senses until Vladimir has patiently explained it all to him, detail by detail. More important, he can remember nothing for two minutes together and can refer back no further than to the last phrase uttered:

v: The tree, look at the tree.
e: Was it not there yesterday?
v: Yes, of course it was there. Do you not remember? We nearly hanged ourselves from it. But you wouldn't. Do you not remember?
e: You dreamt it.
v: Is it possible that you've forgotten already?
e: That's the way I am. Either I forget immediately or I never forget.
v: And Pozzo and Lucky, have you forgotten them too?
e: Pozzo and Lucky?
v: He's forgotten everything!

It is as though a great fog of boredom enveloped every event and every word the instant it occurs or is uttered. Estragon's reply to each appeal to common sense and experience is a variation of "Don't ask me. I'm not a historian," while Vladimir's despairing refrain is "Try and remember," or "Do you not remember?" But perhaps Estragon's forgetfulness is the cement binding their relationship together. He continually forgets, Vladimir continually reminds him; between them they pass the time.

It also keeps them talking, which is essential to their minimal sanity:

v: We always find something, eh, Didi, to give us the impression that we exist?
e: Yes, yes, we're magicians. But let us persevere in what we have resolved, before we forget.

The sound of their own voices keeps back the swaddling cloud of unknowing and reassures them of their own existence, of which they are not otherwise always certain since the evidence of their senses is so dubious. They are, in fact, in constant need of a reassurance they never get. When Pozzo reappears in Act Two he cannot remember meeting them the day before. The little boy who is Godot's messenger flatly denies ever having seen them before. Just before he makes his first exit Vladimir asks him anxiously, "You did see us, didn't you?" as though he, too, were not certain. And well he might be uncertain, because the boy remembers nothing of them on his next appearance. Again Vladimir asks him as he leaves, "You're sure you saw me, eh, you won't come and tell me tomorrow that you never saw me before?" But it is a question without hope, like all the others.

The tramps have another reason to keep talking; they are drowning out those voices that assail them in the silence, just as they assailed nearly all Beckett's other heroes:

E: In the meantime let's try and converse calmly, since we're incapable of keeping silent.
V: You're right, we're inexhaustible.
E: It's so we won't think.
V: We have that excuse.
E: It's so we won't hear.
V: We have our reasons.
E: All the dead voices.
V: They make a noise like wings.
E: Like leaves.
V: Like sand.
E: Like leaves.
   Silence.
V: They all speak together.
E: Each one to itself.
   Silence.
V: Rather they whisper.
E: They rustle.

v: They murmur.
e: They rustle.
    Silence.
v: What do they say?
e: They talk about their lives.
v: To have lived is not enough for them.
e: They have to talk about it.
v: To be dead is not enough for them.
e: It is not sufficient.
    Silence.
v: They make a noise like feathers.
e: Like leaves.
v: Like ashes.
e: Like leaves.
    Long silence.
v: Say something!
e: I'm trying.
    Long silence.
v (*in anguish*): Say anything at all!
e: What do we do now?
v: Wait for Godot?
e: Ah!

There is an important difference between the voices murmuring in the novels and those heard by Vladimir and Estragon. The droning of the Unnamable is interminable, self-absorbed to the point of breakdown and unreadability. In comparison, the voices heard by the *clochards* have, in Frank Kermode's words, "rotted down into images"; what the audience hears are not the voices but their effects. This concentrates them, solidifies them, brings them closer.

In a curious way the first-person narrator of Beckett's novels seems consistently less personal and human than the figures on the stage into whom the same preoccupations are projected. This is not simply because the plays use live actors—after all, Beckett has done his best to overcome this disadvantage by burying them in urns, sand, and dustbins. Rather, it has to do with the quality of the writing. There is nothing in any of Beckett's prose or verse so sharp, immediate, and alive with suggestion as there is in his writing for the stage and radio. I suggested earlier that the further he went from formal verse, the more essentially poetic his work became. It is in the purity and concentration of his dramatic writing that he achieves his real poetry. But since he has always been a man obsessed by voices, perhaps it is only natural that he should need the instrument of the human voice in order to express his genius in its fullest form.

The tramps' duet on "all the dead voices" is a brilliant and wholly original piece of theatrical writing. The theme expands and echoes back on itself, each stage being announced—"All the dead voices," "They all speak together," "They talk about their lives"—briefly developed, then expanded into images chastely, with an absolute discipline of the ear. This combination of austerity straining against imaginative wealth would make it, isolated from the rest of the play, as good a poem in its own right as anything written at that time. This is another facet of Beckett's importance in modern literature: without quite seeming to, he has forced a way through to authentic poetic drama. The conventional, sub-Elizabethan inflation of Drinkwater and Fry led nowhere, except back to Thomas Otway. Eliot had seemed to be opening new ground in *Sweeney Agonistes*, but he abandoned the project; in his later plays, despite his absorption in the technical problem of breaking up the traditional iambic pentameter, he managed to do little more than add a dimension of spiritual portentousness to the world of Terence Rattigan. In comparison, Beckett seems far less grandiose; he uses knockabout routines—falling trousers and swopping hats—which come straight from the world of Laurel

and Hardy. Yet he ends with plays that are genuinely
poetic, both in dramatic conception and in language;
they make their effect like poems, immediately and
elliptically, through a language at once stripped to its
essentials and yet continually stirring with life. Above
all, his imagination seems to range more freely and
supplely once he has cut it loose from the constraints
of his novels' self-regarding gloom.

Beckett's genius, however, has never been inclusive
or wide-ranging. On the contrary, it is like a laser beam,
narrow, intense, and continually probing deeper and
deeper into the same tight area of darkness. In a way,
the essay on Proust is a blueprint for everything he
has done since, although its turgid style gave no hint
of his subsequent power. Thus *Godot* begins with a
series of echoes from the earlier works, as though all
the usual notes had to be sounded before the play could
move off into its own world. According to the stage
directions, Vladimir comes on "with short, stiff strides,
legs wide apart" like the "headlong tardigrade" of Watt,
Belacqua, and the unnamed hero of "The Expelled." In
his opening speech Vladimir remarks: "All my life I've
tried to put it from me, saying, Vladimir, be reasonable,
you haven't yet tried everything. And I resumed the
struggle." Molloy's closing words are: "Well, I suppose
you have to try everything once, succour included, to
get a complete picture of the resources of their planet.
I lapsed down to the bottom of the ditch." A ditch, in
fact, is where Estragon has spent the night, just as
Watt also passed time in one. Two pages later Vladimir
remarks: "One of the thieves was saved. It's a reasonable percentage." Malone says the same: "Why be dis-
couraged, one of the thieves was saved, that is a gen-
erous percentage." Immediately after, Vladimir suggests that he and Estragon should have repented like
the thief:

E: Repented what?

V: Oh . . . (*He reflects.*) We wouldn't have to go into details.

E: Our being born?

That is an echo of *Malone Dies*, which in turn echoes one of the basic themes of *Proust*: namely, that to be born is the original sin.

There are many other echoes from earlier works. Pozzo is Moran writ large and dramatic—bullying, sadistic, orotund, much given to little rituals of comfort and self-indulgence. Pozzo has Lucky chained to him by a rope; Moran contemplated the same fate for his son. Both Pozzo and Moran end "falling to bits," helpless and despairing. When Lucky thinks out loud, his great speech is abstract, theological, full of bogus learned references.[1] He sounds like the Unnamable run amuck. No Joycean stream of consciousness for him; his speech is a masterpiece of unfinished, unfinishing, and unfinishable logic. Its subject is God's dubious mercy, which so exercised Belacqua Shuah.

There are two other great speeches, both at the end of the play, both variations on the same theme and both focusing on the same image:

POZZO: Have you not done tormenting me with your accursed time? It's abominable. When! When! One day, is that not enough for you, one day like any other day, one day he went dumb, one day I went blind, one day we'll go deaf, one day we were born, one day we'll die, the same day, the same second, is that not enough for you? They give birth astride of a grave, the light gleams an instant, then it's night once more.

[1] These include at least one private joke: Cunard is cited several times as a learned authority. Nancy Cunard was Beckett's first publisher and gave a prize to *Whoroscope*, which is as abstract, learned, and theological as anything Lucky manages.

Moments later Vladimir echoes Pozzo's words as he broods over the sleeping Estragon:

> v: Astride of a grave and a difficult birth. Down in the hole, lingeringly, the grave-digger puts on the forceps. We have time to grow old. The air is full of our cries. (*He listens.*) But habit is a great deadener.

Both are speeches of great resonance and conviction, Beckett at his most powerful. Yet they also repeat the same theme and the same image as the young Beckett once pompously expanded in his diatribe against the "Time cancer" and the monstrous tyranny of Habit:

> The creation of the world did not take place once and for all time, but takes place every day. Habit then is the generic term for the countless treaties concluded between the countless subjects that constitute the individual and their countless correlative objects. The periods of transition that separate consecutive adaptations (because by no expedient of macabre transubstantiation can the grave-sheets serve as swaddling-clothes) represent the perilous zones in the life of the individual, dangerous, precarious, painful, mysterious and fertile, when for a moment the boredom of living is replaced by the suffering of being.

Apparently, the only real change in Beckett's thinking over all those years is in understanding that the "macabre transubstantiation" of swaddling-clothes into grave-sheets does, in fact, take place. Otherwise, it is the same image and the same predicament: Pozzo and Vladimir have both entered "the perilous zone . . . when for a moment the boredom of living is replaced by the suffering of being." Neither likes what he sees, but both know there is nothing to be done. "On!" cries Pozzo to Lucky as they make their last exit. "You must go on, I can't go on, I'll go on," says the Unnamable. "I can't go on," repeats Vladimir. "I can't go on," says Estragon in his turn. And Vladimir answers, "That's what you think."

Beckett's habit of repeating the same themes and images and even characters from work to work is a strong way of emphasizing that this, and this only, is how it is in his world; whatever the cast, whatever the situation, there is nothing beyond habit, boredom, forgetfulness, and suffering. In other words, "no symbols where none intended." This is why the many and elaborate interpretations that have been foisted on *Godot* seem particularly superfluous. Pozzo and Lucky may be Body and Intellect, Master and Slave, Capitalist and Proletarian, Colonizer and Colonized, Cain and Abel, Sadist and Masochist, even Joyce and Beckett. But essentially and more simply, they embody one way of getting through life with someone else, just as Vladimir and Estragon more sympathetically embody another. "At this place, at this moment of time, all mankind is us, whether we like it or not," says Vladimir, and like many of his comments it is two-edged: "this place" is also the stage on which he is acting. A little later Estragon pays Pozzo a similar compliment: "He's all mankind." It is a gloomy thought, considering Pozzo's blind and raging obduracy, and Estragon is speaking ironically. But in the situation on stage at that moment he is also speaking the truth. In the same way, the inscrutable Mr. Godot is what his name implies: just another diminutive god like all the other little gods—some divine, some political, some intellectual, some personal—for whom men wait, hopefully and in fear, to solve their problems and bring point to their pointless lives, and for whose sake they sacrifice the only real gift they have, their free will. "We've lost our rights?" asks Estragon. "We've waived them," Vladimir replies.

It needs, in short, no allegorist to understand *Waiting for Godot* as the fullest statement of the problem that has bedeviled Beckett, as it bedevils nearly everyone else: how do you get through life? His answer is simple and not encouraging: by force of habit, by going on despite boredom and pain, by talking, by not listening to the silence, absurdly and without hope. On these terms Christ was lucky, unlike Belacqua's lobster, because "where he was it was warm and dry. . . . And they crucified quick." Beckett and his ramshackle cast in rain-sodden northern Europe have a longer, chillier wait. That is why the tramps continually flirt with the idea of suicide and look back nostalgically, almost tenderly, to the time when Estragon threw himself into the Rhone. They know now that such quick and easy solutions are no longer available to them. When they try to hang themselves the rope breaks and Estragon's trousers fall down. All they can do, the only virtue they can exercise, is to continue: "We are not saints, but we have kept our appointment. How many people can boast as much?" And how many playwrights have put such a simple truth so powerfully, so wittily, and so unanswerably?

ENDGAME

Waiting for Godot contains so many echoes of Beckett's work in other forms that it seems, with hindsight at least, to have been implicit all along, although the genius that transformed early tedium into brilliant theater could never have been predicted. But after *Godot* the links with the past drop away as Beckett moves off into his own special orbit. His launch into inner space followed the solution of a specific technical problem: how to overcome gravity and inertia; that is, how to keep an audience interested in his own preoccupation with the boredom and pointlessness of life. In *Godot* his solution was a ritual of question and answer made necessary and kept going by chronic for-getfulness. By the time he wrote *Endgame*, about seven years later, his dramatic technique had become more sophisticated and varied. His poet's ear for the exact nuance and weight of every word had been transformed into a dramatist's equivalent of absolute pitch: an un-canny sense of the ellipses and elisions of talk, the gaps between words, those pauses and silences which work on stage to create tension and meaning.

Godot took place on a country road at evening when the tramps, like Molloy and Moran, had ceased their wandering. *Endgame* is played out in a single room, like *Malone Dies*. Of the four characters, only Clov can move. He has the usual stiff-legged gait and is unable to sit down, like Cooper, the seedy private eye in *Murphy*. His master, Hamm, is blind and paralyzed in a wheel-chair. Hamm's parents, Nagg and Nell, are legless and dumped in dustbins. When the curtain rises, both Hamm and the bins are covered with dust-sheets, like furniture in a closed house, and the curtains are drawn across the two small windows high up in the rear wall. Clov's first act is to draw back the curtains, peer derisively at the world outside, and then take off the dust-sheets. "This," says Hugh Kenner, "is so plainly a metaphor for waking up that we fancy the stage, with its high peepholes, to be the inside of an immense skull."[2] This perception goes a long way toward explaining the curious shut-in power, authority, and consistency of the play.

The clue Beckett himself provides leads, not sur-prisingly, more or less nowhere. The title suggests a game of chess and Hamm prefaces each development of the nonplot by announcing, "Me to play." But this is little more than one of those devices by which Beckett habitually upstages his own seriousness. (He is also,

[2] Kenner, *Samuel Beckett* (London, 1962), p. 155.

apparently, a chess fiend.) The real "old endgame lost of old" is that of life, "lost of old," because, however subtle the intermediate moves, death's final checkmate is inevitable. "It is no longer," says Alain Robbe-Grillet, "a case of man affirming his position, but of submitting to his fate."[3] In *Endgame* there is no mysterious Mr. Godot who might, if he ever arrived, resolve the protagonists' problems. There is, in fact, no one at all waiting in the wings; all the components of the tragifarce are present when the curtain goes up, like the forces locked tight in each man's skull.

Murphy, Beckett's first thoroughgoing solipsist, pictured his mind "as a large hollow sphere, hermetically closed to the universe without. This was not an impoverishment, for it excluded nothing that it did not itself contain." Later, Murphy finds his mind's ideal objective correlative in the padded cell where "the tender luminous oyster-grey of the pneumatic upholstery, cushioning every square inch of ceiling, walls, floor and door, lent colour to the truth, that one was a prisoner of air." This sounds like the setting of *Endgame*: "Bare interior. Grey light." Inside this closed cerebral world the characters submit to a fate the reluctantly active Murphy aspired to: a sterility and immobility reflecting the devasted, "corpsed" world outside.

Although all four characters are even further along Beckett's usual road to terminal deprivation than Vladimir and Estragon, they remain in touch with what they have left behind. The tramps remember almost nothing—even yesterday is too far off for Estragon—so they palliate their present nullity by verbal rituals and vaudeville routines. In comparison, Hamm and his crew may no longer have any more to lose than the *clochards*, but they are sharply aware of what they

[3] *Snapshots & Towards a New Novel* (London, 1965), p. 127.

have already lost. Like the narrators of the trilogy, Hamm and Nagg make efforts to pass the time by telling stories, continually interrupting themselves to comment on their performance, like actors at a rehearsal. But against this is set a counterpoint of reminiscence in which everyone joins. Nell reminds Nagg of their amorous youth when they rowed on Lake Como: "It was deep, deep. And you could see down to the bottom. So white. So clean." Nagg reminds his son of how he used to cry for him in the night. Clov recalls livelier days when he used to plead with Hamm for a bicycle. Hamm himself remembers "all those I might have helped," including Mother Peg when she "was bonny once, like a flower of the field." He also tells a long, much rehearsed story about a man who crawled to him once out of the surrounding desolation, pleading for himself and his child. He tells it as if it were a fiction, like all the other stories, made up to pass the time, but it sounds convincingly like a description of how Clov first arrived at his house. In other words, they all remain in vague touch with a time before the world began to "stink of corpses," when things still happened and they and their emotions still stirred.

The poignancy of the play depends on this continual tension between a lost world of feeling, once known and still yearned for, and the devastated present. Because of this, *Endgame* becomes, in its odd and small-scale way, genuinely tragic, despite the elements of farce and, more important, despite its limitless negation. In Beckett's earlier work the gloom was equally impenetrable, but it was self-enclosed, with no before or after. This is why his heroes seem invulnerable in their anguish, as though they have never had a childhood. It puts them beyond tragedy, which can exist only when there is the knowledge of something valuable that has been irredeemably lost. But in *Endgame* glimmerings of this knowledge are continually, pain-fully present to all four players. When Hamm makes his speech about the mad painter who looked at the world and saw only ashes, he is also describing his own present state, except that he is now blind and uses Clov to look for him onto a world from which all life has been eliminated. Clov, in turn, repeats the same message in his closing speech:

> They said to me, That's love, yes yes, not a doubt, now you see how . . . easy it is. They said to me, That's friendship, yes yes, no question, you've found it. They said to me, Here's the place, stop, raise your head and look at all that beauty. That order! They said to me, Come now, you're not a brute beast, think upon these things and you'll see how all becomes clear. And simple! They said to me, What skilled attention they get, all these dying of their wounds . . . I say to my-self—sometimes, Clov, you must learn to suffer better than that if you want them to weary of punishing you—one day. I say to myself—sometimes, Clov, you must be there better than that if you want them to let you go—one day. But I feel too old, and too far, to form new habits. Good, it'll never end, I'll never go. Then one day, suddenly, it ends, it changes, I don't understand, it dies, or it's me, I don't under-stand that either. I ask the words that remain—sleep-ing, waking, morning, evening. They have nothing to say. I open the door of the cell and go. I am so bowed I only see my feet, if I open my eyes, and between my legs a little trail of black dust. I say to myself that the earth is extinguished, though I never saw it lit. It's easy going. When I fall I'll weep for happiness.

Both Clov's speech and Hamm's represent Beckett's own situation as a writer. He is, when he wants, vividly aware of "The sails of the herring fleet! All that loveli-ness!" but is continually shying away from it: "He'd snatch away his hand and go back into his corner.

Appalled. All he had seen was ashes. He alone had been spared." But spared from what? Clov gives the answer when he says, "you must learn to suffer better than that." The madman had been spared from what the young Beckett called "the suffering of being," the whole world of unprotected feeling from which he so effectively defended himself with obsession, logic, and language. Yet for the practicing artist with a flourishing private creation to his credit—however bleak and deliberately chewed up that creation might be—nihilism in the end is not enough. So traces of the man who observes and responds with extraordinary originality remain buried, like a prehistoric settlement, beneath the broken rubble of talk he fastidiously amasses.

If Kenner is right in thinking that the stage setting is like that of a gigantic skull, then the play itself is a way of representing what goes on in the internal world of a man suffering from chronic depression, like Hamm or the mad painter or all those other madmen whose cause Beckett so urgently espoused in his novels. This is why this work survives on even less plot than *Godot*. It is simply a day in the life of a man at the end of his tether, a man with only his pain-killer to look forward to and his memories to look back on. It is a day like any other day, except that finally the days have accumulated into a life. Clov announces this in his opening speech:

> Finished, it's finished, nearly finished, it must be nearly finished. Grain upon grain, one by one, and one day, suddenly, there's a heap, a little heap, the impossible heap.

Hamm takes this up again toward the end:

> Moment upon moment, pattering down, like the millet grains of . . . (*he hesitates*) . . . that old Greek, and all life long you wait for that to mount up to a life.

Since this is literally an endgame, he has to kill off the forces that make up his world and keep him going. For the purposes of drama the components of his mind are split up into four characters: first, Hamm at dead center—he insists on it obsessionally—a blind and paralyzed bully who prides himself on his despair and helplessness, is secretly guilty about his lack of pity for others, yearns for death, and is most happy when lying obliterated beneath his bloody handkerchief, "old stauncher" of pain as well as blood; second, Clov, a slave who performs for him the bodily actions necessary to keep life going, who gets him up, does his chores, provides biscuits, tonics, and pain-killers, who is unable to rest, since he cannot sit down, and is linked to his master by "a kind of great compassion"; third and fourth, Nagg and Nell, two mutilated and abused parents, kept like so much rubbish in dustbins, who have in common a few memories, a sweet tooth, and their absurd amorousness; by the end, their bin lids are screwed down tight, the mother is dead, the father weeping and moribund. The eyesocket windows give onto a desert, a leaden tideless sea and a gray light over all, "Light black. From pole to pole." In other words, "All he had seen was ashes," a world as it might be after an atomic holocaust. Once again, Beckett has created an image of the appalled, motionless world of catatonia, but this time, unlike in the novels, he has done so without any mannerist symptoms. As a result, what starts as solipsism ends with those vague intimations of nuclear disaster which impinge on everyone's anxieties. So Hamm speaks of his desolate room as a "shelter" and says, "Outside of here it's death," a statement that holds as true for a nuclear survivor as for a chronic depressive. Perhaps this is one reason why the play has exerted such a powerful grip on the imagination of audiences far larger than might ordinarily be expected to respond to its bleakness and condensation.

There are also the extenuating circumstances of the stage. Even more than the narrators of the novels, Beckett's actors are aware of their false position as objects in a work of art and strenuously try to maintain their poise by pre-empting the audience's response. When Vladimir goes off stage to relieve himself, Estragon calls after him, "At the end of the corridor, on the left." Vladimir replies, "Keep my seat." Similarly, Clov at one point turns his telescope on the audience and says, "I see . . . a multitude . . . in transports . . . of joy. That's what I call a magnifier." Hamm, too, has his share of critical comments: "This is deadly," "Not an underplot, I trust"; near the end he turns furiously on Clov as though tired of all their pretense: "An aside, ape! Did you never hear an aside before? I'm warming up for my last soliloquy." It is, I suppose, yet another of Beckett's ways of keeping a decent distance between himself and what might otherwise seem statements of indecently personal intent. But however aware the characters may be of the roles they are playing, and however much they insist on puncturing the theatrical illusion for the audience, the fact that they are there on stage means that the desert of depression is, albeit reluctantly, peopled. The depression has moved out of the bodiless, claustrophobic, pointless world of mere language and assumed the qualifying substantiality of flesh and blood. In the novels Beckett's wit was self-regarding, concerned exclusively with its own learning and elegance. In the plays it ranges easily over the broader absurdity of the characters' gloom and bodily functions. It becomes human instead of literary.

Perhaps this is why *Endgame* admits at the close a faint possibility of hope. The last time Clov looks out the window, in order to reassure Hamm that nothing moves on "this muckheap," he sees to his disgust a small boy. (In the French version the child is sitting on the ground, staring at his navel; in the English there are no details.) Hamm rejects the possibility of a life elsewhere, but uses it as his cue for dismissing Clov:

HAMM: If he exists he'll die there or he'll come here. And if he doesn't . . .
Pause.
CLOV: You don't believe me? You think I'm inventing?
HAMM: It's the end, Clov, we've come to the end. I don't need you any more.

There is a vague, unresolved possibility left hanging in the stale air that the boy may be like the child in Hamm's own unended story, another Clov come to help him in his helplessness. It may be, in fact, that life does go on, despite appearances, and that there is another game of chess still to be played. This brief, perhaps delusory, glimpse of the child is, however, less important to the plot than to the tone. It means that the play ends with a tiny flicker of light in the otherwise unrelieved gloom. It is as though the new energy released in Beckett when he turned to the drama, and evident in the extraordinary skill, wit, and originality of the plays, were somehow changing, even lightening, the quality of his previously unchangeable depression.

KRAPP'S LAST TAPE

The people in *Endgame* differ from Beckett's earlier characters in having a past to look back on. Two years later, in 1958, when he came to write *Krapp's Last Tape*, memory and the contrast between a lost past and the sour present had become Beckett's only themes. The stage and the action are correspondingly bare: an old man alone in a funnel of light, sitting at a table, listening to a tape of himself talking thirty years before. The stage directions decree that he should have the clothes and the look—"White face. Purple nose."—of a senile clown. Appropriately, the brief script is padded out with a good deal of clownish stage business: bananas—he is addicted to them—are ritually peeled and eaten, and one is stuck in his waistcoat pocket; there is much popping of corks and sounds of drinking whenever he disappears into the darkness at the back of the stage, and a good deal of hanky-panky with keys, table drawers, and spools of tape; at one point he even slips on a banana-skin. No doubt the business is necessary in order to make a stage play out of a work that would function, and has, equally effectively as radio. But when a dramatist as subtle and skillful as Beckett milks a laugh by making a man slip up on a banana-skin, there is cause for suspicion. It is as though he were determined to make Krapp ridiculous at any price, not out of contempt but in order to cauterize the feelings that are about to be presented.

As usual, the action is simple: after the introductory business the old man plays a reel of tape he recorded years before, when he was thirty-nine—about the age Beckett was when he settled down to the long stint of work that made him famous. The tape is a retrospect of a year just past and records the death of his mother, mixed with memories of a beautiful nursemaid, a dog, and a rubber ball. There is also a moment of revelation at night by the sea's edge during an equinoctial storm, the storm and darkness apparently reflecting some truth of his inner life. But what that "never to be forgotten" vision was we are not told since the old man is bored by the younger Krapp's youthful pretensions and keeps skipping the tape forward. He is trying to find a scene described in the ledger, in which he summarizes the contents of each reel, as "Farewell to Love." Having found it, he then records his own latest retrospect of the past year. His present style lacks the fluency and precision of his youth. It is starker, more acid and dislocated, as befits a life falling to bits with age and failure. In place of the young man's vision, compounded "of storm and night with the light of the understanding and the fire," he reports a bleaker, deprived reality: "What's a year now? The sour cud and the iron stool." He now lives a life of total obscurity, in both senses of the term: only seventeen copies of the "opus magnum" he had predicted in his moment of truth have been sold and he scarcely leaves his darkened room. As for his love life: "Fanny came in a couple of times. Bony old ghost of a whore. Couldn't do much." His only solace is to lie in bed and dream about his infinitely remote childhood:

> Lie propped up in the dark—and wander. Be again in the dingle on a Christmas Eve, gathering holly, the red-berried. Be again on Croghan on a Sunday morning, in the haze, with the bitch, stop and listen to the bells. And so on. Be again, be again. All that old misery. Once wasn't enough for you.

He sounds like the voices perpetually rustling in the ears of Vladimir and Estragon:

v: What do they say?
e: They talk about their lives.
v: To have lived is not enough for them.
e: They have to talk about it.
v: To be dead is not enough for them.
e: It is not sufficient.

Apparently, once really wasn't enough for Krapp, for he then plays again the dissonant idyll of his "Farewell to Love," picking it up in the middle of his description of his girl and himself drifting in a punt on a summer's day:

> TAPE:—gooseberries, she said. I said again I thought it was hopeless and no good going on and she agreed, without opening her eyes. (*Pause.*) I asked her to look at me and after a few moments— (*pause*)—after a few moments she did, but the

eyes just slits, because of the glare. I bent over
her to get them in the shadow and they opened.
(*Pause. Low.*) Let me in. (*Pause.*) We drifted in
among the flags and stuck. The way they went
down, sighing, before the stem! (*Pause.*) I lay
down across her with my face in her breasts and
my hand on her. We lay there without moving.
But under us all moved, and moved us, gently, up
and down, and from side to side.
Pause. KRAPP's *lips move. No sound.*
Past midnight. Never knew such silence. The earth
might be uninhabited.
Pause.
Here I end this reel. Box—(*pause*)—three, spool—
(*pause*)—five. (*Pause.*) Perhaps my best years are
gone. When there was a chance of happiness. But
I wouldn't want them back. Not with the fire in me
now. No, I wouldn't want them back.
KRAPP *motionless staring before him. The tape
runs on in silence.*

The play ends there and the last sentence of the tape
is the key to it. For the young man who made the
recording it is an affirmation of strength: he has had
his vision, the fire is in him and he knows what he
must do, even if it involves a "Farewell to Love." But
for the old man listening motionless in the darkness
it is an ironically ambiguous echo of his own dessicated
renunciation: "Once wasn't enough for you." In the
end, "all that old misery"—again "the suffering of
being"—*is* in fact too much for him. So he defends
himself against it by drink, bananas, and slapstick.

Yet the beauty of the writing, each spare detail
adding a new dimension of awareness and feeling, pulls
against old Krapp's wisdom of deprivation. And he repeats the passage, so there can be no mistaking the
power of the past. Earlier in the play the younger man
has asked, "Did I sing as a boy? No. Did I ever sing?

No." But that is precisely what he goes on to do in his description of the love scene: "We lay there without moving. But under us all moved, and moved us, gently, up and down, and from side to side." It is one of the few instances in Beckett's work in which anyone admits to being moved, even if only by water, and the rhythm of the language reflects the sense. By repeating the passage and letting the play end with it. Beckett is both undermining the force of old Krapp's denial and emphasizing the magnitude of his loss.

It is a new tone and a new direction for Beckett's writing. All his earlier work is about depression in its various manifestations, from mere boredom to near catatonia, with appropriate attendant symptoms. In comparison, *Krapp's Last Tape* is far more human, open, and available. Its subject is not depression but grief, and instead of shying away from its causes, it shows, poignantly and with great beauty, precisely what has been lost. It stands in the same relation to his other work as what Freud called "mourning," a painful but natural human emotion experienced by everyone, stands in relation to the mental sickness of "melancholia." "Memory and Habit are attributes of the Time cancer." In *Krapp* Beckett for once puts aside the defenses of Habit, allows Memory its due, and becomes vulnerable to the malignant disease of Time. And by some curious creative transformation he emerges with what he had sought unsuccessfully at the start of his career: an allusive, shifting prose equivalent of lyric poetry, despite his accidie, despite his taste for deprivation, despite, perhaps, himself.

EH JOE

Beckett's one television play, produced by the BBC in 1966, is a kind of X-ray photograph of *Krapp's Last*

Tape: the bare bones of a narrative and a language reduced to its essentials, each detail working precisely in its place, at once poignant and abstract. It is also *Krapp* turned inside out, a similar story but from the girl's point of view. Finally, it is a dramatic version of all those voices that so haunted Beckett's other heroes, the voices described antiphonally by Vladimir and Estragon, but never before heard speaking for themselves. Krapp had come closest, but it was his own voice that pursued him. In *Eh Joe* we hear the other voices insidiously at work at last. Joe himself does not speak. Indeed, after the opening moments when he moves about his room, closing the window, drawing the curtains, locking the door and the cupboard, peering under the bed, always with his back to camera, he does not move. We do not see his face until his rituals are complete and he feels, apparently, safe. By this time he is sitting on his bed, "relaxed, eyes closed." He stays like that for the rest of the play, in ever in- creasing close-up, intently staring at the camera while a woman's neutral voice—"Low, distinct, remote, little colour, absolutely steady rhythm, slightly slower than normal," according to the directions—relentlessly ac- cuses him.

Perhaps what she says is a clue to the negation and depression of the other works, for the burden of her voice is guilt, Joe's guilt:

> You know that penny farthing hell you call your mind . . . That's where you think this is coming from, don't you? . . . That's where you heard your father . . . Isn't that what you told me? . . . Started in on you one June night and went on for years . . . On and off . . . Behind the eyes . . . That's how you were able to throttle him in the end . . . Mental thuggee you called it . . . One of your happiest fancies . . . Mental thuggee. . . . Otherwise he'd be plaguing you yet . . . Then your mother when her

hour came . . . "Look up, Joe, we're watching you" . . .
Weaker and weaker till you laid her too . . . Others . . .
All the others . . . Such love he got . . . God knows
why . . . Pitying love . . . None to touch it . . . And
look at him now . . . Throttling the dead in his head.

All those who loved him once and whom he had done
down return one by one as voices from the dead to
haunt him. He has to kill them a second time in his
head, thereby compounding his guilt. It is a treadmill
from which there is no escape, because it is a projection
of the "penny farthing hell" he calls his mind. In other
words, *Eh Joe* is Beckett's most intimate and precise
image of the anguish he has devoted most of his creative life to describing: a man shut off on his own in a
sealed room, tortured by an unforgiving multitude of
voices. This is like the world of the schizophrenic which
Murphy, in his innocence, admired and yearned for.
But now it is presented in its full horror, from the
inside.

The horror is redeemed only by the seductiveness of
the writing, which brings it close and yet, at the same
time, makes it curiously tolerable. This is clearest at
the climax when the woman's unwavering voice repeats the story of her predecessor who also loved Joe
but, unlike her, didn't get away:

All right . . . Warm summer night . . . All sleeping . . . Sitting on the edge of her bed in her lavender
slip . . . You know the one . . . Ah she knew you,
heavenly powers! . . . Faint lap of sea through open
window . . . Gets up in the end and slips out as
she is . . . Moon . . . Stock . . . Down the garden
and under the viaduct . . . Sees from the seaweed
the tide is flowing . . . Goes on down to the edge and
lies down with her face in the wash . . . Cut a long
story short doesn't work . . . Gets up in the end sop-
ping wet and back up to the house . . . Gets out the
Gillette . . . The make you recommended for her

body hair . . . Back down the garden and under the viaduct . . . Takes the blade from the holder and lies down at the edge on her side . . . Cut another long story short doesn't work either . . . You know how she always dreaded pain . . . Tears a strip from the slip and ties it round the scratch . . . Gets up in the end and back up to the house . . . Slip clinging the way wet silk will . . . This all new to you, Joe? . . . Eh Joe? . . . Gets the tablets and back down the garden and under the viaduct . . . Takes a few on the way . . . Unconscionable hour by now . . . Moon going off the shore behind the hill . . . Stands a bit looking at the beaten silver . . . Then starts along the edge to a place further down near the Rock . . . Imagine what in her mind to make her do that . . . Imagine . . . Trailing her feet in the water like a child . . . Takes a few more on the way . . . Will I go on, Joe? . . . Eh Joe? . . . Lies down in the end with her face a few feet from the tide . . . Clawing at the shingle now . . . Has it all worked out this time . . . Finishes the tube . . . There's love for you . . . Eh Joe? . . . Scoops a little cup for her face in the stones . . . The green one . . . The narrow one . . . Always pale . . . The pale eyes . . . The look they shed before . . . The way they opened after . . . Spirit made light . . . Wasn't that your description, Joe? . . .

Like many other passages in Beckett, this has the sharpness and economy of poetry and yet remains narrative, taking the listener efficiently from one point of time to another. In terms of the medium, it is also wholly original. In a sense, it had to be, for there was no way in which Beckett could otherwise have accommodated the alien form of television to his overriding obsession with the inner world. The essential characteristic of both film and television is that everything should be subordinate to the eye; the audience is made to see not only with their eyes, but also with their ears and minds, absorbed into a compelling alternate reality which, at its best, is as immediate and engulfing as a dream. In these circumstances a highly literary script, which might work perfectly on the stage, would be somehow distracting. The writing would draw attention to itself in a situation in which everything should be subordinate to the image.

Beckett's solution was to stand the usual procedure on its head, making the language itself take over the function of the camera. After the neutral opening sequence when Joe moves about his room, the camera simply holds him in close-up, gradually moving in four inches at a time, as though further into his skull, as the savage accusations pile up. Instead of varying the visual images, Beckett makes the language itself continually cut from one detail to another in a kind of verbal montage. In this way, even his most elegant, hard-won writing—"Moon going off the shore behind the hill . . . Stands a bit looking at the beaten silver"—reinforces the cinematic effect instead of interrupting it, just as a particularly beautiful image in a film at once adds to one's pleasure and makes one attend, provided it is absorbed into the whole and not insisted upon. Alexandre Astruc, the French film critic, described the New Wave of film-makers as wielding *"le caméra stylo"*: that is, they use the camera as naturally and unselfconsciously as a writer uses his fountain pen. Beckett has reversed that. In *Eh Joe* he is using a *stylo caméra*: creating a visual multiplicity of images, sensations, associations, and narrative with his language alone, while the television camera itself holds one unvarying shot.

PLAY

Three years before *Eh Joe*, Beckett had used a variation of this montage technique in his remarkable *Play*, first performed in Germany in 1963. In this case the montage was not of images and impressions, but simply of the narrative: the same story is told from three points of view, each broken into meshing but contrasting fragments.

On one level, *Play* is a dramatic version of *The Unnamable*: set in some kind of afterlife where the protagonists—a man, his wife, and his mistress—are encased in urns, their heads fixed immovably, their faces, according to the stage directions, "*so lost to age and aspect as to seem almost part of urns.*" As usual, all they can do is talk. But they speak only in response to the probing of an invisible, voiceless interrogator—a spotlight, in fact, set in the footlights—switching abruptly from one to another, shutting them off, starting them up haphazardly, always when they are in full flow, sometimes even in the middle of a word.

The stories the Unnamable told and his unstoppable, monotonous dissection of despair were a means of distraction, keeping the horror of his situation at bay. In *Play*, what the characters say is their torment; if they were allowed to stop talking they would find the silence and darkness they long for. Instead, the piercing light, like an evil version of the Beatific Vision Dante saw in Paradise, makes them retell their sordid little story endlessly. Literally so, since the play is repeated a second time without variation. It is like Sartre's *Huit-Clos*, but without any conventional trimmings—concentrated, fierce, and abrupt. Their own special hell is an eternal playing out of a vicious triangle, again and again, without respite, in what one of them calls "hellish half-light." They all sense that their mute, dispassionate interrogator wants something of them. The wife thinks it may be penitence, the mistress madness. The man, who is both more stupid and more weary, simply knows that there is some truth hidden in him which will not out; he has a fantasy of them all drifting together in a little dinghy, like Krapp and his girl; so maybe the truth is love. More likely, all three are expiating without end the guilt of having lived. So the man yearns for the time when "all this" that he suffers now will be, like his adultery, "just play." Whence the work's ambiguous title.

Compared with the allusive verbal montage of *Eh Joe*, the writing is plain, the narrative direct, however fragmentarily it emerges as each protagonist tells his part antiphonally, at the bidding of the blank eye of light. But because the plot itself is conventional, it picks up a certain power and centrality that much of Beckett's work lacks. Adultery, after all, has been the great theme of the European novel from *La Princesse de Clèves* and *Adolphe* through *Le Rouge et le Noir*, *Madame Bovary*, and *Anna Karenina* down to *Le Diable au Corps* and *Lady Chatterley's Lover*. In *Play* Beckett uses that tradition and extends it into his own particular preoccupation with hell and despair. The result is to make the latter seem natural instead of gratuitous and excessive, as it so often does. More important, it means that the play is sustained not by Beckett's usual name-less, faceless anguish but by a precisely focused personal viciousness and a fierce undercurrent of sexual anger. As always, the language is clean and cool, but it trembles with violence and disgust. For example, the mistress's description of her first meeting with the wife:

> One morning as I was sitting stitching by the open window she burst in and flew at me. Give him up, she screamed, he's mine. Her photographs were kind to her. Seeing her now for the first time full length in the flesh I understood why he preferred . . . What are you talking about? I said, stitching away. Some-one yours? Give up whom? I smell you off him, she screamed, he stinks of bitch.

There is the same canny mixture of cliché, hatred, and repulsion in the man's description of his reconciliation with his wife:

> At home all heart to heart, new leaf and byegones byegones. I ran into your ex-doxy, she said one night, on the pillow, you're well out of that. Rather un-called for, I thought. I am indeed, sweetheart, I said, I am indeed. God what vermin women. Thanks to you, angel, I said.

This stew of angry contempt and fetid sexuality is the real substance and theme of the play. It makes the urns and the intimations of a distasteful immortality, which belong to a convention Beckett has made his own, seem altogether less compelling than the other, older tradition of adultery, which may be more commonplace but is also more human and more urgent. In his later work *Play* is the only exception to the claustrophobic rules Beckett has made for himself out of his own idiosyncratic preoccupations. But for precisely that reason it is also one of his most powerful pieces of writing, adding a savage cutting edge to that vision of post-humous torment Beckett has always been obsessed with. The first of all his heroes was named Belacqua, after an amiable, passive, more or less tolerated in-habitant of purgatory. In contrast, the characters in *Play* are in real hell; their sin is lust and hatred, not sloth, and their torments proportionately agonizing. It is a pity that this most available of Beckett's plays should be so rarely performed.

HAPPY DAYS

Happy Days, written in English between 1960 and 1961, is the most cheerful play Beckett has written and the least interesting. It is also the most theatrical in the specialized, technical sense of the term. It has only two characters, a middle-aged couple called Winnie and Willie. Winnie is buried in sand and unable to move, Willie does not emerge fully until the end. For the rest of the time only the back of his bald head is visible or he is out of sight; he has very little to say for himself. As a result, Winnie has to hold the audience on her own, by her voice and her facial expression, in one long maundering solo. It is, as they say, a supremely testing vehicle for an actress.

The play is also theatrical in the other sense that distinguishes, as Beckett's plays usually do not, between literature and pure theatre. It has little of Beckett's bleak purity of language; instead, it is simply a text for acting, full of those weird verbal and visual running gags that work so well in performance, but nevertheless make for dull reading. For example, for much of the first act Winnie tries to read the writing on the handle of her toothbrush; "Fully guaranteed genuine pure" is perfectly clear, but what follows is hard to make out. For page after page of text the audience is kept on tenterhooks for her to say "bristle." It never happens. What she finally deciphers is "Hog's setae." It is a typically Beckett pedantic joke; Belacqua Shuah or Murphy would have been proud of it. It also prompts Winnie's henpecked, scarcely speaking, scarcely visible husband to his most passionate speech:

> WINNIE: What *is* a hog, Willie, please!
> WILLIE: Castrated male swine. (*Happy expression appears on* WINNIE's *face.*) Reared for slaughter. (*Happy expression increases.*)

To both of them, apparently, this seems a fair description of himself, since his wife replies ecstatically: "Oh this *is* a happy day! This will have been another happy day!"

As usual, Beckett spikes the audience's guns by having Winnie describe a vulgar couple, the "last human kind to stray this way," who had peered at her incredulously as she lay half-buried. The husband voices the audience's objections, the wife gives the author's replies:

> What's she doing? he says—What's the idea? he says—stuck up to her diddies in the bleeding ground—coarse fellow—What does it mean? he says—What's it meant to mean?—and so on—lot more stuff like that—usual drivel—Do you hear me? he says—I do, she says, God help me—What do you mean, he says, God help you? And you, she says, what's the idea of you, she says, what are you meant to mean?

It is a strong way of saying "no symbols where none intended." Even so, no symbol hunting is needed to see the play as a sour view of a cozy marriage: a monosyllabic, gently bullied husband, with his straw boater, newspaper, and dirty postcard, and an iron but sentimental wife who wakes and sleeps to order, prays, preens, and rabbits on unstoppably about the happy days she has known. She consoles herself, while she still has the use of her arms, by rummaging in a shopping bag full of improbable oddments, everything from a toothbrush to a revolver. Her favorite phrase is "That's what I find so wonderful." She is the opposite of all those chronic complainers on whom Beckett elsewhere lavishes so much sympathy. On the evidence of the play, he finds her and her manic defenses ludicrous at best.

As though to prove that cheerfulness is no better rewarded than despair, he gives her the full standard treatment. In Act One she is buried to the waist in earth; by Act Two she is up to the neck, unable to move her head in any direction. Yet she remains, to the bitterest end, implacably optimistic and talkative.

It is a comic version of the Unnamable's final anguish—
"I can't go on, I must go on, I'll go on"—acted out by
someone who, in the face of both the evidence and the
rising earth, can still find nothing to complain of
and no reason for not going on or for silence.

Beckett is too subtle a writer to make Winnie merely
a figure of fun. The flow of her maundering and her
constant variation between schmaltz and steely self-
righteousness is controlled with immense skill. He also
allows her associate membership of his elect by making
her hear voices, although—sensible to the end—she
rationalizes them:

> Sometimes I hear sounds. But not often. They are a
> boon, sounds are a boon, they help me . . . through
> the day. The old style! Yes, those are happy days,
> when there are sounds. I used to think . . . I say I
> used to think they were in my head. But no. No no.
> That was just logic. Reason. I have not lost my
> reason. Not yet. Not all. Some remains. Sounds. Like
> little . . . sunderings, little falls . . . apart. It's
> things, Willie. In the bag, outside the bag. Ah yes,
> things have their life, that is what I always say,
> *things* have a life.

It is a mark of Beckett's perfect ear for dramatic pitch
that this unexpected and unprepared for irruption of
elements from another eerier world is absorbed unhesitatingly into her suburban prattle. Yet despite his
skill, awareness of nuance and humor—maybe even
because of them—the play seems, in the end, to labor
a single point at inordinate length. He is deliberately
creating a play out of nothing at all, continually raising
obstacles for himself in order to show how brilliantly
he can overcome them. The technical problems involved
in sustaining a two-act drama—with one actress buried
in the center of the stage and another only a vague
presence off—are absurdly difficult, his solution to them

effortless: literally, a case of "Look, no hands." So the play demonstrates at length his mastery of the art of theater; but it does very little else, apart from reiterating the gritty conviction he seems to have been born to: blessed are the optimists, for they shall be buried alive.

Radio: Christ What a Planet!

●

IV

For a writer who has continually created characters haunted by voices, radio is a natural medium. In a sense, everything Beckett has written has been devoted to the task of catching the precise speed and cadence of the voices in his head. That is the essence of his scrupulousness with language and that extraordinary accuracy of ear which allow him to combine elegance with colloquialism; it also probably explains his undisguised boredom and impatience with the demands of conventional narrative and plot. These latter count for so little that his stage plays lose little of their force when broadcast with appropriate sound effects. Even the novels might be made into effective radio if there were an audience patient and devoted enough. He is one of the rare examples of a writer whose work maintains an unflagging literary excellence and yet is dominated by the spoken voice and the ear.

ALL THAT FALL

Beckett wrote his first radio play, *All That Fall*, in 1956, the same year he completed *Fin de Partie*. He wrote it in English, the first time he had used the language since finishing *Watt* in 1945. Perhaps this is why the work has links with the mannered world of Irish character he had already left behind him. The cast includes a whole gallery of local peasantry and dignitaries—Christy, a carter; Mr. Tyler, a retired bill-broker; Mr. Slocum, Clerk of the Racecourse; Tommy, a porter; Mr. Barrell, a stationmaster; Miss Fitt, a lady in her thirties—who accompany Mrs. Rooney on her slow and complaining journey to the local station. They garrulously pass the time of day and serve, in their different ways, as foils to her grumbling. Mr. Slocum squeezes her with vast effort into his car; Tommy squeezes her out of it again, with equal difficulty; Miss Fitt supports her as she labors up the station steps. Her journey is shorter than Molloy's, but scarcely less painful.

Mrs. Rooney is hardly in a condition to travel, being in her seventies, quivering and derelict, "two hundred pounds," says her husband, "of unhealthy fat." He, in turn, is equally decrepit and also blind. She meets him at the train on which he commutes daily from his haven in town, his "silent, backstreet, basement office, with its obliterated plate, rest-couch and velvet hangings," where he is "buried . . . alive, if only from ten to five, with convenient to the one hand a bottle of light ale and to the other a long ice-cold fillet of hake. Nothing, I said, not even fully certified death, can ever take the place of that." He shares this lugubriousness with his wife, whose talk is also studded with gems of the death wish: "It is suicide to be abroad. But what is it to be at home, Mr. Tyler, what is it to be at home? A lingering dissolution." In their different ways, both husband and wife are still mourning the loss of their daughter, little Minnie, who died as a child. Mr. Rooney is sour and clenched up on himself in grief; his "grandchildless" marriage is an extended penance. His wife is more histrionic, regularly given to spasms of sorrow when, as she puts it, "it all came flooding over her again." That first death has transformed both of their lives into nothing more than a long day's dying.

Their gloom, however, is so excessive that Beckett milks it cannily—at least at the beginning of the play—for pure comedy. Mrs. Rooney is made into one of those women whose only satisfaction is in the sicknesses, operations, and bereavements they have endured. Her keening is continually parodied both by her own soap opera and also by the sounds of an irrepressible nature—birds, sheep, cows, wind, rain—a nature made deliberately intrusive by courtesy of the special effects department.

In a way, Beckett could do little else except parody his own habitual depression, given the gallery of grotesques he wheels into action. It is as though the cast of *Murphy* had suddenly appeared in the closing pages of the trilogy (which, in turn, would be like casting the Marx Brothers in a play by Eugene O'Neill). Beckett, of course, is far too self-aware an artist to believe that his own prescriptions for despair could sound anything but funny when rolled out by a cast of stage Irish. More important, the broad comedy of the start is a way of making palatable the play's altogether more acid and somber close.

Mrs. Rooney has waited at the platform, noisy with her imagination of disaster provoked by the lateness of the train. It arrives at last and, as she and her husband toil painfully home, he indulges in a long and inconclusive narrative of his journey. The train had stopped between stations; he is careful not to say why. This immediately prompts his wife to a seemingly irrelevant story of her own:

MRS. R: I remember once attending a lecture by one of these new mind doctors. I forget what you call them. He spoke—

MR. R: A lunatic specialist?

MRS. R: No no, just the troubled mind. I was hoping he might shed a little light on my lifelong preoccupation with horses' buttocks.

MR. R: A neurologist.

MRS. R: No no, just mental distress, the name will come back to me in the night. I remember his telling us the story of a little girl, very strange and unhappy in her ways, and how he treated her unsuccessfully over a period of years and was finally obliged to give up the case. He could find nothing wrong with her, he said. The only thing wrong with her as far as he could see was that she was dying. And she did in fact die, shortly after he washed his hands of her.

MR. R: Well? What is there so wonderful about that?

MRS. R: No, it was just something he said, and the way he said it, that have haunted me ever since.

MR. R: You lie awake at night, tossing to and fro and brooding on it.

MRS. R: On it and other . . . wretchedness. When he had done with the little girl he stood there motionless for some time, quite two minutes I should say, looking down at his table. Then he suddenly raised his head and exclaimed, as if he had had a revelation, The trouble with her was she had never been really born! He spoke throughout without notes. I left before the end.

MR. R: Nothing about your buttocks? (MRS. ROONEY *weeps.*)

Although Beckett is careful to insulate the seriousness of what Mrs. Rooney has to say—whence the jokes
about horses' buttocks and the ineffectual fumbling for
the word "psychoanalyst"—this is as straight a statement as he has ever allowed himself of the malaise
at the heart of his work. Like the little girl who died
because she had never been really born, like himself
as a young critic of Proust, all his characters are not
depressed for any particular reason; they are depressed
because they are alive, which, in turn, means they will
eventually die. In his later years Freud came to view
the psyche as a battleground for an unending struggle
between the pleasure principle and the death instinct.
In Beckett's work the death instinct wins; it is as
though the force of life were too fragile and uncertain
to withstand the overwhelming pull toward death.
Beckett's ambiguous achievement in the trilogy was to
create an art form in which he could inhabit his own
death. On the evidence of Mrs. Rooney's extraordinary
speech, life had never offered him any compelling
alternative.[1] But in the trilogy he spoke of life as the
original sin for which there is no atonement; here he
makes the same point without the protective theologiz-
ing. Hence the title of the play, which is taken from the
text of a sermon soon to be preached at the Rooney's
local church: "The Lord upholdeth all that fall and
raiseth up all those that be bowed down." According
to the stage directions, the Rooneys respond to this
with an outburst of "wild laughter."

[1] According to Peggy Guggenheim, Beckett himself once
had a fantasy rather like that of never being really born:
"Ever since his birth, he had retained a terrible memory of
life in his mother's womb. He was continually suffering from
this and had awful crises, when he felt he was suffocating."
(*Confessions of an Art Addict* [London, 1960], p. 50). Beckett
may, of course, simply have been testing Miss Guggenheim's
credulity.

Like *Godot*, the play ends with a young boy bringing a message; or rather, he comes on an errand from the stationmaster, but ends as a messenger when Mrs. Rooney asks him why the train was delayed: "It was a little child fell out of the carriage, Ma'am. On to the line, Ma'am. Under the wheels, Ma'am." Those are the last words of the play. Grief is starting up in another corner of this convulsed universe for another couple much like the Rooneys. Earlier in the play Mrs. Rooney had cried out in despair, when no one would help her up the station steps, "Christ what a planet!" At the time, it was just another comic exaggeration. By the end of the play it seems, like the wild laughter at the consolations of religion, the only appropriate response.

EMBERS

All That Fall is the richest, most brilliant, but also most conventional of Beckett's works for radio. After it there were no more characters in the ordinary sense, only voices and sounds coming out of the air, disembodied and insidious. There were, in fact, no more radio *plays*, only pieces for voices, as precisely scored and as abstract as musical compositions, at best variations on dramatic themes that never quite freed themselves from their creator's skull.

Embers, written and broadcast in English in 1959, takes the first necessary leap into a solipsism as thoroughgoing as Murphy's. It concerns a man called Henry, who wanders alone on a beach, talking and talking to drown out the impossible sound of the sea. He summons up ghosts (of his father who does not speak, of his wife who does), tells stories, peremptorily commands sounds (the noise of hooves, for instance) which begin and end at his bidding, listens to brief flashbacks from the bullied life of his daughter whom he never liked; in short, he tries everything to obscure, however briefly, the sea's eternal complaint.

As his wife makes clear in the course of their imaginary conversation, this is an old obsession of his. He has spent a lifetime talking loudly and dementedly to himself, terrifying his own child in the process. But from his point of view this was better than talking to those around him: "Ada too, conversation with her, that was something, that's what hell will be like, small chat to the babbling of Lethe about the good old days when we wished we were dead."

Like many of Beckett's heroes, Henry's main defense against the intolerable, demanding reality of other people and of the sea is to tell stories. He tells one on and off throughout the piece, carefully modifying the phrasing, developing details, but never actually finishing it. It is about two old men in a silent, darkened house, both "fine old chaps, very big and strong," standing before the fading embers of a fire. Outside the world is frozen, "bright winter's night, snow everywhere, bitter cold, white world, cedar boughs bending under the load," and inside the fire is dying. Bolton is "an old man in great trouble"; Holloway is his friend, a doctor, whom he has called for help. (Holloway, we are told, is also the name of Henry's doctor.) But what kind of help he wants Bolton will not say. He only peers into Holloway's face and says, "Please! PLEASE!" He is seeking, presumably, the same "kind of great compassion" that kept Clov caring for Hamm despite every abuse. He needs, in short, companionship in his great trouble.

So, too, does Henry, forever talking, forever calling up his ghosts:

Stories, stories, years and years of stories, till the need came on me, for someone, to be with me, anyone, a stranger, to talk to, imagine he hears me, years of that, and then, now, for someone who . . . knew me, in the old days, anyone, to be with me, imagine he hears me, what I am, now. No good either.

So he calls up his dead and tells a story which repeats the same need in a different way. But this is also the predicament of every writer, particularly a writer as solitary as Beckett, who had deliberately shut himself up for five or six years while he wrote stories about men shut in their rooms writing stories. It is a long way from the early confidence of the essay on Proust:

> For the artist, who does not deal in surfaces, the rejection of friendship is not only reasonable, but a necessity. Because the only possible spiritual development is in the sense of depth. The artistic tendency is not expansive, but a contraction. And art is the apotheosis of solitude. There is no communication because there are no vehicles of communication.

Even at this earliest point in his literary career Beckett understood something Joyce and his contemporaries missed: that the purer the artistic effort, the more ineluctably it led not to impersonality, but to inner "spiritual" depths. Yet there comes a point of contraction where solitude and the depths are no longer bearable. Beckett's devotion to the principle of contraction has been unwavering; each work is stripped more and more of its inessentials until all that remains is a kind of archaic shorthand, the runes of despair. But the human pressures this process must create seem at moments to have become intolerable. The tighter the solipsist's universe closes in on him, the more sharply he allows the works to protest. But he does not cheat. Henry in his own "great trouble" remains a solipsist, beyond friendship and help; the people he summons, like the hooves, have no existence outside his own head. The only external reality is the sound of the sea, which he can neither tolerate nor escape, a tormenting ground bass to a deprived life burning, like the fire in Bolton's house, down to its embers.

Embers is a condensed dramatic statement of the difficulties of being a writer. The two subsequent radio pieces treat a similar subject, but from a different angle—not the disproportionate human cost of creation, but the process itself.

In *Words and Music*, written in English in 1961, the process is acted out by three characters: Croak, a poet, and his two servants, Words and Music, whom he calls Joe and Bob. At the beginning Music, a small orchestra, is tuning up while Words proses on repetitively, abstractly, polysyllabically, and unpunctuated about that old favorite of Beckett's, sloth. Croak shuffles in and brings them to order with a club. The theme tonight, he announces, is Love. Words immediately repeats his same dull prosing, substituting Love for Sloth. Croak is anguished. He summons Music to try for something more appropriate, but with no greater success. Croak tries cajoling them and Words responds with some grandiose rhetoric. Croak's anguish increases. Again Music manages nothing better. Croak suggests another theme, Age, and becomes more agonized and more violent in his rejection of his two servants' paltry attempts. Very gradually, protestingly, Words and Music clear their throats of hesitations, platitudes, and periphrases. A poem tentatively emerges, phrase by phrase, Words and Music helping each other on until both are softly singing together. Finally, the first two themes, Love and Age, are brought successfully into unison: an old man with his old love to tend him. The next stage is the particular: "The face," Croak commands. This time there are fewer hesitations, although Words lapses quickly into polysyllabics when allowed his head. In the end, the poem is finished, subtle, touching, precise, and, incidentally, better than almost any of the poems Beckett has published on their own. Croak abruptly drops his club and shuffles away, leaving Words pleading with Music to repeat his part of the work that has cost them both so much.

It is a brilliant, witty, utterly original dramatization of the labor and frustrations of creation, the poet alternatively bullying and despairing, his instruments inept, unwieldy, and only slowly, despite themselves, becoming usable; then the final letdown when there is nothing more to be done. It also illustrates vividly that split between the music the poet hears in his head and the leaden words at his command, and the slow, unwilling process of disciplining and refining these two elements until they finally chime together in a single work of art. From Coleridge to Mayakovsky poets have described, later and from a distance, the various ways in which they piece poems together line by line. But to my knowledge only Beckett has managed to make a work of art out of the struggle of making a work of art.

Cascando, written in French in 1962, treats the same theme from a slightly different angle—creating prose not poetry—and in a considerably bleaker and more fragmented style. Instead of Croak with his club and slippers, his bullying and wheedling, there is only a tight-lipped Opener who commands Voice and brings in Music as it suits him. Voice is the eternal Beckett narrator, whipping himself on to tell just one more story in the vain hope that it will be the unattainable right one that, when finished, will allow him to rest in silence. In other words, *Cascando* is a reduced, abstract version of the novels and involves the same old story: Woburn a derelict in the standard Beckett uniform—old overcoat and hat—staggering on his motiveless way to the sea, continually collapsing in the mud and heaving himself up again, staggering on, Voice ever more desperate and fragmentary, until Woburn finally drifts out to sea in an open boat, like the tramp in an earlier story, "The End," or Macmann, whose story Malone is telling as he dies. And while Voice stumbles on like Woburn, sustained by Music, gradually weakening, urged violently on by Opener—"Come on! Come on!"—Opener himself ponders on why he bothers, in his turn, to blunder on opening and closing stories that are never quite what he is after:

> What do I open?
> They say, He opens nothing, he has nothing
>   to open, it's in his head.
> They don't see me, they don't see what I do,
>   they don't see what I have, and they say, He opens
>   nothing, he has nothing to open, it's in his head.
> I don't protest any more, I don't say any more,
>   There is nothing in my head.
> I don't answer any more.
> I open and close.

This is the last judgment on all that solipsistic muttering that has persisted in Beckett's work, from the elegant Mr. Endon through volume after volume of increasingly anguished whispering. The charge is that this is not art but madness: "They say, He opens nothing, he has nothing to open, it's in his head." It is a charge the Opener prefers not to answer; instead, he continues to do what he must: "I open and close." Beckett says the same thing using other words in the last of his "Three Dialogues with Georges Duthuit":

> To be an artist is to fail, as no other dare fail, that failure is his world and the shrink from it desertion, art and craft, good housekeeping, living. . . . I know that all that is required now . . . is to make of this submission, this admission, this fidelity to failure, a

new term of relation, and of the act which, unable to act, obliged to act, he makes, an expressive act, even if only of itself, of its impossibility, of its obligation.

Cascando is in itself an "expressive act," a dramatization of the artist's "fidelity to failure." So Opener, driven on by the hope of resting after a last "right" story, is faithful not to his inner voices but simply to his function: "I open and close."

Cascando is less witty and dramatic than *Words and Music* and pursues a less satisfying quarry: not a finished poem, but a story that is, as it has to be, broken and unending. Even so, it dramatizes once again a complex, agonized aesthetic in a peculiarly direct way. This is typical of Beckett's curiously diversified yet monolithic achievement. He has played variations on remarkably few themes, not extending his range, but refining it. What makes him such a creative figure is the originality with which he restates the same case in unexpected ways, so that what is familiar is transformed into something new and unpredictable.

Later Works: Imagination Dead

V

The narrowness of Beckett's range, the way the same themes are repeated and transfigured from work to work until the whole corpus seems like a single block of marble—smooth, white, but with intricate veins of color connecting each area with all the others—is unusual in a writer of his stature. His unassailable reputation among both experts and the general public is, it would seem, a tribute to his continual search for a special kind of perfection, a perfection manifest in his unfailing stylistic control and economy of language, his remorseless stripping away of superfluities. It is also an acknowledgment of the persistency with which he has been true to his own black lights: he began depressed, worked his way through to an art that expressed that depression poignantly and in a multitude of ways, and has rarely deviated from his logic of denial. He is like a painter whose distaste for the excesses of style and the claims of the imagination make him end with a blank canvas. Beckett's play *Breath* is as near that final nullity as a practicing dramatist can decently get, and the pieces of prose that precede it do much the same for the novel. Although in their original French versions they were each published separately, they are all shorter than most short stories: *Imagination Dead Imagine* and *Ping* run to about a thousand words each; *Enough* and *Lessness* are about two thousand; *The Lost Ones* is an epic in comparison, about seven and a half thousand words.

Enough, first published in French in 1966, is the least interesting. It concerns yet another pointless pilgrimage, begun when the narrator was six and continuing for some ten years, with a man so aged that he moved with his body jackknifed through ninety degrees. This improbable pair walked hand in hand "several times the equivalent of the terrestrial equator. At an average speed of roughly three miles per day and night." The old man murmured intermittently and almost inaudibly; the younger listened. They occupied most of the slow eternity in their companionship with that old consoler of Beckett's obsessionals, mental arithmetic:

> We took flight in arithmetic. What mental calculations bent double hand in hand! Whole ternary numbers we raised in this way to the third power sometimes in downpours of rain.

They lived off flowers and slept wedged together; the weather was nondescript. Finally, the young man left his companion just short of the crest of a rise and never saw him again, a gesture of independence which seems to him now, in his own decrepitude, a disgrace. And that is all. It is a vague sketch for an idea—on the interdependence of age and youth, perhaps—that leads, literally, nowhere.

In comparison, the other works have a good deal more power and purpose. Each is a vision of some kind of Dantesque afterlife. *Imagination Dead Imagine* came first—published in French in 1965—and its subject is precisely what its title says: imagine a world in which the imagination is dead. For Beckett, all that remains is a white rotunda almost invisible in the surrounding whiteness. From the outside the sphere seems solid as a skull, "a ring as in the imagination the ring of bone," but far larger. In fact, it is hollow, and Beckett provides precise internal measurements— "diameter three feet"—and geometrical coordinates to go with them. Enclosed within this rotunda are two white bodies, one male, one female, lying on their sides in the fetal position, back to back, head to arse. He uses the coordinates to plot the precise position of their limbs. The light pulses between white and black and, as it does so, the temperature changes from hot to freezing. Occasionally, although only once together, one or the other figure opens its blue eyes and stares unblinkingly. An "infinitesimal shudder" and a faint murmur show that they are neither dead nor sleeping. Otherwise, there is no movement, only the pulsing change from hot white to frozen black, through gradations of gray. It is the last image of a dying imagination, itself a proof that the imagination is not yet dead: a fertilized, stillborn egg, or an almost dead star lost in orbit. The writing is like stage directions, tight-lipped, condensed, and to the point, meticulously detailed as to measurements, the duration of the changes in light and heat and the positions of the bodies, each in its own hemisphere. It is a terminal vision of a world become motionless and colorless, yet still, despite everything, faintly living. "Hold a mirror to their lips, it mists"; the echo of King Lear's words emphasizes the distance between Shakespeare's universe and Beckett's. The devastated, postatomic landscape outside the skull room of *Endgame* has been reduced to this tiny mori-bund sphere lost in white space, a last image for the imagination to cling to in an inner space as blank as that between the galaxies.

Ping, all that remains of a novel begun late in 1965, manipulates much the same properties: a single white, bare body, this time upright, in a rectangular white box measuring one yard by two by one, like a capacious coffin. Only the vague blue of the figure's eyes—"only just light blue almost white"—disturbs the engulfing whiteness. Otherwise, he is featureless and closed up: "Nose ears white holes mouth white seam like sewn invisible," "legs joined like sewn." Occasionally, there is a faint, brief murmur, more rarely a fainter, briefer flash of memory. But it is misleading to describe the work in this narrative way, as if there were in fact a plot. Instead, there are only descriptive elements jammed together in sentences without syntax and con-stantly repeated. As in *How It Is*, Beckett uses a prose beyond grammar, playing variations on a handful of words to produce a single frozen image. It is neither a novel nor a poem, but a kind of minimal verbal con-struction.

So, too, is *Lessness*, first published in French in 1969, although it manages to be both more explicit and more plaintive. The color now is ash gray: a little rigid gray body in a landscape of gray ruins, gray sand, gray sky. This is the "true refuge" from the blinding light and symmetry of the previous two works: "Four square all light sheer white blank places all gone from mind." But the figure in this monochrome landscape suffers faint stirrings of emotion, yearning for a time when he was still sufficiently alive to curse God and be un-happy: "Old love new love as in the blessed days un-happiness will reign again." He also remembers, or imagines, a living world of rain, blue sky, and the cycle of the days: "Figment dawn dispeller of figments and the other called dusk." In other words, the rigid little figure is not simply observed from the outside, like his predecessors, as an evidence of life in an otherwise sterile universe. Despite his ash-gray world, he has memories of a quicker, more vulnerable existence which make him yearn for final oblivion: "Blacked out fallen open four walls over backwards true refuge issueless." Or, the clotted syntax being difficult to focus, the figure is at least a channel through which feelings can flow. And this vague stir of life and emotion, as though from a huge distance, is reflected in the elliptical beauty of the language. It is the last, distant echo of those tender descriptions of nature Beckett occasionally allowed himself, despite his avowed distaste, in the trilogy. Given a depression less overpowering and a less single-minded determination to express it, Beckett might have created a peculiarly rich, precise, and peopled world. Instead, he has devoted himself to images of deprivation on which he has brought to bear not only a disproportionate inventiveness, but also a piercing awareness of how much has been lost. *Lessness* is a microscopic but perfect model of this continual tension between feeling and nullity, life and death, which lies at the heart of all his work.

The Lost Ones was written in 1966, before *Ping* and *Lessness*, although the last paragraph was not added until 1970. Like the rest of the late prose, it is a vision of purgatory, but busier, more conventional and also considerably less allusive. This time purgatory is "a flattened cylinder fifty metres round and eighteen high" into which are crammed two hundred "lost bodies," each searching restlessly for its mate, like the two sundered halves of Plato's egg. They mill about at the center of the cylinder or slowly shuffle in Indian file around the central crowd, peering at those who queue in the outermost zone by the walls, where they wait their turn to climb ladders. These ladders give the climbers a view of the crowd from above or take them to one of the niches and tunnels that honeycomb the cylinder walls. The light is yellowish; the temperature oscillates every four seconds between hot and cold. Apparently, the lost ones will never find what or whom they are searching for. In the end they will simply give up and join the blind ranks of the "vanquished." This does not mean they will die, since death is a blessed state rarely attained in Beckett's world; they will simply cease from activity, give up their quest, like Molloy and Moran. When all have done so, the cylinder will come to rest, the light and temperature stop pulsing, and there will be peace at last.

Beckett describes all this in straight, rather long-winded prose which has only one peculiarity: all commas have been omitted. This is the reverse of his procedure in his earlier novels which were so peppered with commas that every sentence became an infinitely receding series of qualifications. Leaving the commas out is no less tiresome a mannerism, and it does not disguise the unusual pomposity of the language:

> Here is the reason why this in reality infrequent infringement whether on the part of those who push on up to the niches and tunnels or of those who halt on the way never gives rise to the fury vented on the wretch with no better sense than to climb before his time and yet whose precipitancy one would have thought quite as understandable and consequently forgivable as the converse excess.

This reads like a report by a civil service commission inquiring into the conditions in purgatory. It harmonizes well enough with Beckett's perennial obsession with the mathematics of every detail—surface area of the cylinder, shifts of temperature, length of ladders, and so on—but it is a long way from the concentration and purity of his other late pieces. It sounds like Words's preliminary stumbling orotundities before Croak brings him to heel with his club; that is, like some rough draft Beckett might eventually reduce and mold into proper poetic shape.

Beckett, however, is far too careful and costive a writer ever to publish anything he has not worked over endlessly. In the past few years he has released his minimal late works in the way De Beers releases diamonds: sparingly, almost grudgingly, in order not to ruin the market. So there can be no question of *The Lost Ones* being simply a mistake, at least as far as Beckett himself is concerned. Instead, it is yet another attempt in yet another style to pin down the vision of sterile desolation that has always haunted him. At one point, those of the "little people" who have temporarily given up their fruitless search are compared obliquely to Dante's Belacqua. So perhaps one motive for the work is to ask how that oldest of Beckett's heroes looks forty years later. The inevitable answer is he looks as faceless, purposeless, and defeated as ever.

This is an echo of Beckett's own fate, as all his latest works make clear in their different ways. He is a novelist, possessed by the need to tell stories, who has nevertheless done his best to kill off the novel as a viable form, reducing it to a few pages of spare prose in which the same phrases are repeated and repeated and the whole world is stripped away until only a single image is left, immobile in a neutral light. He is also a master of dramatic dialogue who has worked steadily to reduce his plays to the condition of silence.

Beckett's first attempt to achieve this perverse absolute was *Come and Go*, written in English early in 1965. Three women sit in a circle of light on a dark stage. Their ages are "undeterminable," their faces shrouded by their hat brims, their hands apparently unadorned. They are joined by a shared but distant past, "in the playground at Miss Wade's," where they would sit together "on the log" much as they are sitting together still. But between past and present a lifetime of desolation has intervened and death now has his hooks in all three. When each in turn moves out of the circle of light—silently, on rubber soles—the remaining two come together on their bench:

> FLO: Ru.
> RU: Yes.
> FLO: What do you think of Vi?
> RU: I see little change. (FLO *moves to centre seat, whispers in* RU'S *ear. Appalled.*) Oh! (*They look at each other.* FLO *puts her finger to her lips.*) Does she not realize?
> FLO: God grant not.

This exchange is repeated with variations three times as each of the three women comes and goes from the light to the shadows. All are doomed, but each is determined to protect the others from the destructive knowledge. So they sit unspeaking, "dreaming of love" and "of the old days. Of what came after." Silence is the only means of preserving the illusions by which they all survive. This is another variant of that "great compassion" Hamm yearned for. But now there are only hints and silences, the ravages of living redeemed by shared memories and shared fictions. At the end they join hands, all three linked together as in a childhood game. The last words of the play are a reminder of other, unshared loves: "I can feel the rings." But for the audience, their hands are bare.

This is the opposite of the vicious circle of *Play*, where each of the three protagonists was tormented by paranoid fantasies of the others' secret pleasures. In *Come and Go* there is only a remote finger-tip protectiveness and mutual illusion, a ritual coming and going from light to dark, and a mutually tender suppression of the knowledge of evil, the pang for what is lost and gone pre-empting the dread of what is to come.

Come and Go lasts about three minutes and employs 121 spoken words. Apparently, even that came to seem excessive to Beckett. *Breath*, first staged in New York in 1969, lasts precisely 35 seconds and dispenses altogether with actors and words.[1] This is the complete text, including all stage directions:

Curtain.

1. Faint light on stage littered with miscellaneous rubbish. Hold for about five seconds.
2. Faint brief cry and immediately inspiration and slow increase of light together reaching maximum together in about ten seconds. Silence and hold about five seconds.
3. Expiration and slow decrease of light together reaching minimum together (light as in 1) in about ten seconds and immediately cry as before. Silence and hold for about five seconds.

Rubbish. No verticals, all scattered and lying.
Cry. Instant of recorded vagitus. Important that two cries be identical, switching on and off strictly synchronized light and breath.
Breath. Amplified recording.
Maximum light. Not bright. If 0 = dark and 10 = bright, light should move from about 3 to 6 and back.

The pun on *inspiration* seems to be unintentional, yet perhaps this is the image Beckett has been searching for all along, his final comment on the human condition: a stage empty of everything except a little rubbish, a dim light never intensifying to real brightness, a

[1] Strangely enough, Beckett originally wrote *Breath* for Kenneth Tynan's revue *Oh! Calcutta!* But the producer characteristically added "including naked people" to the stage directions. Beckett withdrew his piece.

faint birth cry, a single breath in and out, a second faint cry, then silence. So much for life. So much, too, for the ripe prose of the secretary of the Swedish Academy who gave Beckett the Nobel Prize: "In the realms of annihilation, the writing of Samuel Beckett rises like a Miserere from all mankind, its muffled minor key sounding liberation to the oppressed and comfort to those in need." The only Miserere Beckett has ever uttered is for those burdened with the compulsion to write, the only liberation he is interested in is from the oppression of language.

In that context, *Breath* seems inevitable. If an author devotes a lifetime to writing about deprivation in all its forms—material and emotional, the hoboes and the certifiable—then, if he is consistent, he finishes with a work of art deprived of art. Just how deprived is clear if one compares *Breath* with a passage from that other master of despair, Kierkegaard:

Listen to the newborn infant's cry in the hour of birth—see the death struggles in the final hour—and then declare whether what begins and ends in this way can be intended to be enjoyment.

True enough, we human beings do everything as fast as possible to get away from these two points, hurry as fast as possible to forget the birth-cry and change it to delight in having given a being life. And when someone dies we immediately say: Softly and gently he slipped away, death is a sleep, a quiet sleep—something we do not say for the sake of the one who died, for our talking cannot help him, but for our own sake, in order not to lose any of the zest for life . . . during the interval between the birth-cry and the death-wail, between the mother's shriek and the child's repetition of it, when the child at some time dies.

Imagine somewhere a great and splendid hall where everything is done to produce joy and merriment—but the entrance to this room is a nasty, muddy, horrible stairway and it is impossible to pass without getting disgustingly soiled, and admission is paid by prostituting oneself, and when day dawns the merriment is over and all ends with one's being kicked out again—but the whole night through everything is done to keep up and inflame the merriment and pleasure.

What is reflection? Simply to reflect on these two questions: How did I get into this and this and how do I get out of it again, how does it end? What is thoughtlessness? To muster everything in order to drown all this about entrance and exit in forgetfulness, to muster everything to re-explain and explain away entrance and exit, simply lost in the interval between the birth-cry and the repetition of this cry when the one who is born expires in the death struggle.[2]

In the final analysis, Kierkegaard is no less unswervingly pessimistic than Beckett, he is simply more vulnerable. He is passionate, indignant, willing to risk his poise, as Beckett himself once was when he allowed Pozzo to cry furiously, "They give birth astride of a grave, the light gleams an instant, then it's night once more." But in these late works Beckett is as defended as an armadillo. It is possible that he is saying: Beware, have no illusions; life is only a breath between the birth cry and the death cry. But he may also be saying that life is simply a cosmic yawn. After all, he has labored devotedly to express his depression in a multitude of ways, and the one symptom of depression he has never shirked is boredom—chronic, paralyzing boredom, engulfing everything, particularly the weary profession of writing. From the beginning he has created characters who, in their different ways and at different intensities, have been at their last gasp.

[2] *Søren Kierkegaard's Journals and Papers*, vol. 1, ed. Howard V. Hong *et al.* (Bloomington, Ind., 1967), pp. 338–39.

Breath is, literally, that last gasp. It is difficult to see where Beckett can go on to.

No doubt this is underestimating his resources and unceasingly inventive technique, which has enabled him to make art out of material that in the hands of someone less gifted would have seemed merely a suitable case for treatment. His work is narrow, obsessional, and gloomy, but it is also exceptionally pure. This purity is in his meticulous style, which is bare, self-denying, and consistently refuses every easy solution; it is also in the curious inevitability of his development, which has been as persistently logical and austere as his language.

> Well, thought Belacqua, it's a quick death, God help us all.
> It is not.

He began depressed and has been true to his depression. It took unusual courage and doggedness, as well as great talent, to follow this logic of denial through to its desolate end.

Postscript, 1973

In November 1972, after this essay was finished, *Not I* was staged in New York, then repeated two months later in London. It proves, among other things, the obvious folly of underestimating genius. After the tenuousness and apparent exhaustion of *Come and Go* and *Breath, Not I* is a theatrical event as powerful, despite its mere fifteen minutes' duration, and as unprecedented as *Waiting for Godot* and *Endgame*. It also focuses in one final, unanswerable image all Beckett's lifelong obsessions. Inevitably, it is an image as denuded as a block of ice. On one side of a darkened stage stands a shrouded, silent, mostly immobile Auditor, like a priest listening to a penitent in the confessional; on the other, a single spotlit woman's mouth, high up in the darkness, dementedly talking. Nothing else of the woman is visible. The mouth seems possessed by a separate life of its own, unceasingly pouring out its horrified broken phrases, interrupting itself, occasionally

screaming, occasionally breaking into wild laughter at
the mention of "a merciful . . . (*brief laugh*) . . . God
. . . (*good laugh*)." It is the theatrical equivalent of one
of Francis Bacon's appalled images; a whole world of
anguish squeezed into the tight, white circle of a mouth
gabbling violently on the fine edge of hysteria, as if to
pause would be to expose itself to pressures which
would tear it apart. The mouth mentions a ray of light
coming and going like the Inquisitor in *Play*, demanding some truth the speaker can't get at. It wonders dis-
jointedly if what it is now undergoing is some kind of
divine punishment. Although the audience at first hear-
ing will probably miss—and is probably meant to miss
—a fair proportion of this cascade of words, they combine with the vision of that flickering, bone-white mouth
to create a state of suspended horror as immediate as a
nightmare.

What the mouth says is, like the image, a distillation
of everything Beckett has striven to express in his long
career. Fragment by fragment, continually doubling
back on itself, correcting, repeating, amplifying, always
hurrying, terrified to stop, it tells, as usual, a story. This
time it is the story of a schizzy old woman, an orphan
from birth ("so no love . . . spared that"), who has
passed her seventy-odd years of life more or less in
silence, speaking at most "once or twice a year . . . always winter some strange reason . . . the long eve-
nings . . . hours of darkness . . . sudden urge to . . .
tell . . ." Then one April, picking cowslips in a field,
she is suddenly, without warning or reason, possessed
by the need to speak. Not that she wants to speak or
has anything to say; on the contrary, her brain can
scarcely catch what her mouth says and passionately
resists this avalanche of utterance:

> . . . mouth on fire . . . stream of words . . . in her
> ear . . . practically in her ear . . . not catching the

half . . . not the quarter . . . no idea what she's saying . . . imagine! . . . no idea what she's saying! . . .
and can't stop . . . no stopping it . . . she who but a
moment before . . . but a moment! . . . could not
make a sound . . . no sound of any kind . . . now can't
stop . . . imagine! . . . can't stop the stream . . . and
the whole brain begging . . . something begging in
the brain . . . begging the mouth to stop . . . pause a
moment . . . if only for a moment . . . and no response . . . as if it hadn't heard . . . or couldn't . . .
couldn't pause a second . . . like maddened . . .

It is as though those voices which all Beckett's characters have listened to so intently had taken the old
woman over, imbuing her mouth with a frantic life of
its own while the rest of her body remains as inert and
insentient as it has always been. This is a variation
on Beckett's perennial theme: the speaker's voice is,
in reality, the voice of another speaking to the speaker,
as though there were always some split between the
mouth and the brain, unbridgeable if it were not for
the style itself, which doggedly maintains its thin narrative line in precisely the broken torrent of words it
describes. In a way, *Not I* is the final dramatic expression of the Unnamable's last words and Beckett's
own bleak formulation to Duthuit of his vocation as a
writer:

> The expression that there is nothing to express, noth-
> ing with which to express, nothing from which to
> express, no power to express, no desire to express,
> together with the obligation to express.

But with this difference: instead of will power and
obligation there is now an absolute, immediate, ungain-
sayable need to express.

But it is also a dramatization of the artist's even more
profound predicament. The silent Auditor's four slight
movements come when, as though he had interrupted,
the mouth pauses in its mad tirade and cries:

"What? . . . who? . . . no! . . . she!" Each time the movement the Auditor makes in response to these four words is, according to the stage directions, a "simple sideways raising of arms from sides and their falling back, in a gesture of helpless compassion." The pity he expresses is—again the stage directions—for the mouth's "vehement refusal to relinquish third person." Whence the title, *Not I*: the speaker cannot or will not acknowledge that this agony belongs to her, not to some old madwoman she has invented. And this, perhaps, is also the predicament of Beckett himself as an artist who has gone on telling stories despite his distaste, lack of interest, and minimal gift for narrative, forced both by the nature of the forms he employs and by his own unwavering preference for anonymity to continue with the fiction of making fictions out of what is in fact personal anguish. In a way, the whole gallery of his invented characters, from Belacqua Shuah through all the heroes, named and unnamable, of his novels and plays, are variations on his own "vehement refusal to relinquish third person"; they are ways of affirming in the teeth of experience the two words which will keep the anguish at bay: Not I. On the evidence of this last play, the "I" is still insisting on being heard—luckily for us, since this is, I think, one of the few continually stirring features in the otherwise dreary landscape of contemporary theater.

BIOGRAPHICAL NOTE

1906	Samuel Barclay Beckett born at Foxrock, near Dublin, on Good Friday, April 13, second son of William Frank Beckett, a quantity surveyor, and Mary (née Roe), both Protestants.
1920–23	Educated at Portora Royal School, Ulster.
1923–27	Trinity College, Dublin. Read Modern Languages (English, French, and Italian).
1926	Elected to a Foundation Scholarship in Modern Languages.
1927	B.A., prize and gold medal for outstanding performance in Finals.
1927–28	Taught for two terms at Campbell College, Belfast.
1928	Paris. *Lecteur d'anglais* at Ecole Normale Supérieure. Met James Joyce.
1929	First publications: "Dante . . . Bruno, Vico . . . Joyce" in *Our Exagmination*; short story, "Assumption," in *Transition*.
1930	Published *Whoroscope* (poem) in Paris. Helped translate Joyce's "Anna Livia Plurabelle" into French.
1930–32	Lecturer in French at Trinity College, Dublin. Resigned after four terms.

1931   Published *Proust* in London. M.A. Trinity College, Dublin.

1932   Beginning of five years of wandering in Germany, France, England, and Ireland. Began a novel, *Dream of Fair to Middling Woman* (unfinished and unpublished).

1933   Father died, leaving Beckett a small annuity. Two "bad years" living in Gertrude Street, Chelsea, London, supplementing income by literary journalism and translation.

1934   Published *More Pricks Than Kicks* (stories) in London.

1935   Published *Echo's Bones and Other Precipitates* (poems) in Paris.

1937   Settled in Paris.

1938   Published *Murphy* in London.

1939   Visited Ireland. Returned to Paris at outbreak of war. Began translating *Murphy* into French.

1941–42   Worked in French Resistance with his friend Alfred Péron.

1942   August. Gestapo arrested Péron. Beckett fled from Paris with Suzanne Dumesnil, later his wife. Settled in Roussillon in the Vaucluse in unoccupied France. Began working on *Watt*.

1945   Visited Ireland. Finished *Watt* in Dublin. Worked for Irish Red Cross in Normandy. Returned to Paris. Beginning of his most creative period, writing exclusively in French.

1946–47   Wrote *Mercier et Camier* (novel) and *Nouvelles* ("La Fin," "L'Expulsé," "Le Calmant," "Premier Amour").

1947   Wrote *Eleuthéria* (play, unpublished) and *Molloy*.

1947–48   Wrote *Malone Meurt*.

1948–49   (October 1948–January 1949) Wrote *En Attendant Godot*.

1949   Published "Three Dialogues with Georges Duthuit" in *Transition*.

1949–50   Wrote *L'Innommable*. Translated *Anthology of Mexican Poetry* commissioned by UNESCO.

1950   Beckett's mother died.

1950–52   Wrote *Textes pour rien*.

1951   *Molloy* and *Malone Meurt* published in Paris.

1952   *En Attendant Godot* published in Paris.

1953   First production of *Godot* at Théâtre de Babylone,

Paris, January 5. *L'Innommable* published in Paris. *Watt* published in Paris (in English).

1954   *Waiting for Godot* published in New York.

1955   Published *Nouvelles et Textes pour rien* and *Molloy* (in English) in Paris. Began *Fin de Partie* in December. *Godot* produced in London.

1956   Finished *Fin de Partie*. Wrote *All That Fall* (in English) and *Acte sans Paroles I & II. Malone Dies* published in New York. *Godot* produced in New York and published in London.

1957   Translated *Endgame* into English. *Fin de Partie* published in Paris and produced in Paris and London (in French). *All That Fall* broadcast by BBC and published in London and New York. *Proust* reprinted in New York.

1958   Wrote *Krapp's Last Tape. Krapp* produced and published in London. *The Unnamable* and *Anthology of Mexican Poetry* published in the United States. *Malone Dies* published in London.

1959   *Embers* written (in English) and broadcast on BBC. The trilogy published in New York and in Paris (in English).

1960   Wrote *Comment C'Est*. Began *Happy Days* (in English). *Krapp's Last Tape, All That Fall, Embers and Mimes* published in New York. The trilogy reprinted in London.

1961   Finished *Happy Days*. Wrote *Words and Music* (in English). *Happy Days* staged and published in New York. *Comment C'Est* published in Paris. *Poems in English* published in London.

1962   Wrote *Cascando* (in French). Began *Play* (in English). *Words and Music* broadcast by BBC. *Happy Days* published in London.

1963   Finished *Play*; first performed (in German) at Ulm, West Germany. Wrote scenario for *Film. Cascando* broadcast in France.

1964   *Film* produced, directed by Alan Schneider and starring Buster Keaton. *Play* produced in London and New York, published in London with *Words and Music* and *Cascando. Cascando* broadcast (in English) by BBC. *How It Is* published in London and New York.

1965   Wrote *Eh Joe* and *Come and Go* (in English). *Imagination Dead Imagine* published in English and French in London and Paris. *Proust and Three Dialogues* reprinted in London.

1966   Wrote *Assez* and most of *Le Dépeupleur* (*The Lost Ones*). *Eh Joe* televised by BBC. Published *Ping* and *Assez* in Paris. *Come and Go* produced in Berlin and Paris.

1967   Published *Eh Joe* (with *Film* and *Mime II*), *Come and Go*, and *Ping* in London. Also *No's Knife* (collected shorter prose from *Stories and Texts for Nothing* to *Ping*). *Stories and Texts for Nothing* published in New York.

1968   *Come and Go* performed in London. *Poèmes* (collected French poems) published in Paris.

1969   *Sans* (*Lessness*) published in Paris. *Breath* (originally written for Kenneth Tynan's *Oh! Calcutta!*) published in London, produced in New York and Glasgow. Awarded the Nobel Prize for literature.

1970   *The Collected Works* published in New York. *Lessness* published in London. *More Pricks Than Kicks* reprinted in London and New York. *Le Dépeupleur* finished. *Mercier et Camier* and *Premier Amour* published in Paris.

1971   *Le Dépeupleur* published in Paris.

1972   *The Lost Ones* published in London. *Not I* produced in New York.

1973   *Not I* produced and published in London. *First Love* published in London.

SHORT BIBLIOGRAPHY

Dates of original publication of Beckett's works are given in the Biographical Note. The Grove Press, New York, published *The Collected Works of Samuel Beckett* (1970) in sixteen volumes. Grove and its paperback subsidiary, Evergreen Books, also publish Beckett's works separately. His French publishers are Éditions de Minuit, Paris.

A Samuel Beckett Reader, edited by John Calder (London: Calder & Boyars, 1967) includes a helpful introduction and commentary. A Beckett bibliography is provided in *Samuel Beckett: His Works and His Critics,* edited by Raymond Federman and John Fletcher (Berkeley: University of California Press, 1970).

There is a vast number of books and articles on Beckett. I mention only some of the more useful:

BOOKS
Calder, John. *Beckett at 60.* London: Calder & Boyars, 1967. Personal memoirs, tributes and two critical essays.
Cohn, Ruby. *Samuel Beckett: The Comic Gamut.* New Brunswick, N.J.: Rutgers University Press, 1962.
Federman, Raymond. *Journey to Chaos: Samuel Beckett's Early Fiction.* Berkeley: University of California Press, 1965.

Friedman, Melvin J., ed. *Samuel Beckett Now*. Chicago: University of Chicago Press, 1970. A summary of the state of Beckett criticism, plus essays and a critical checklist.

Kenner, Hugh. *Samuel Beckett: A Critical Study*. New York: Grove Press, 1961; rev. ed. 1973.

ARTICLES

Dennis, Nigel. "The Collected Works of Samuel Beckett," in *New York Review of Books*, vol. 16, no. 6 (April 8, 1971).

Kermode, Frank. "Beckett," in *Modern Essays*. London: The Times, 1971.

Lees, F. N. "Samuel Beckett," in *Memoirs and Proceedings of the Manchester Literary and Philosophical Society* 104 (1961–1962).

Robbe-Grillet, Alain. "Samuel Beckett: On Presence on the Stage," in *Snapshots & Towards a New Novel*. London: Calder & Boyars, 1965.

Tynan, Kenneth. Two reviews of Beckett plays, in *Curtains*. New York: Atheneum, 1961.

INDEX